Confident
PARENTS,
Exceptional
TEENS

Confident
PARENTS,
Exceptional
TEENS

TED HAGGARD & JOHN BOLIN

ZondervanPublishingHouse
Grand Rapids, Michigan

A Division of HarperCollins*Publishers*

Confident Parents, Exceptional Teens
Copyright © 1999 by Ted Haggard and John Bolin

Requests for information should be addressed to:

≣ ZondervanPublishingHouse
Grand Rapids, Michigan 49530

Library of Congress Cataloging-in-Publication Data

Haggard, Ted.
    Confident parents, exceptional teens : creating a teen-friendly family / Ted
Haggard and John Bolin.
        p.   cm.
    Includes bibliographical references.
    ISBN 0-310-23339-9 (softcover)
     1. Parent and teenager—United States. 2. Parenting—United
States. 3. Adolescence—United States. 4. Teenagers—United
States—Family relationships. I. Bolin, John, 1969- .
II. Title.
HQ799. 15.H34 1999
649' . 125—dc21
                                         99-43136
                                           CIP

Interior design by Laura Klynstra Blost

Printed in the United States of America

---

99 00 01 02 03 04 05 /❖ DC/ 10 9 8 7 6 5 4 3 2 1

Contents

PART
One

Kids in Trouble

CHAPTER
One

Kids in Trouble

Life affords no greater responsibility, no greater privilege, than the raising of the next generation.

C. EVERETT KOOP

One day our little boys and girls will grow up. No matter how hard we fight to avoid the inevitable, it happens. We can stick their old crayon drawings back on the refrigerator, and we can hang their handmade clay ornaments from the Christmas tree, but we can't stop the clock. One day our little boys will grow into men and our little girls will grow into women. Gracefully or painfully, happily or resentfully, they will grow up. It's up to us, as parents, to help them determine how.

When our kids are young, it's easy to be full of hopes and dreams for their futures. We long to see the first steps, the first bicycle ride, the first report card, the first best friend, the first kiss. We love long talks in their bedroom and hope they know that they can always come to us with their problems. We live for that sparkle in their eyes or the sound of the door opening when they come in from school. And we look forward to the years to come when they'll proudly bring home their own family to share backyard barbecues and Thanksgiving dinners.

But for many of us, somewhere along the path of life the dreams fade. Our bright little girls suddenly become stiff, inward, and uninterested. Our boys come home with funny, suspicious looks, hanging shoulders, and dragging feet. An awkward but certain distance settles between our teens and us. Instead of laughter there's sarcastic conversation, or even worse, silence. When we notice their childlike admiration being replaced by looks of embarrassment and disapproval, we begin to feel like we don't know them anymore. We don't understand their friends. And worst of all, we have no idea where we went wrong.

Sure, parents have been dealing with troubled teenagers for centuries. But aren't today's teenagers a little different? Aren't they facing issues that we didn't face as teens? Our youth detention facilities are busting at the seams, our juvenile courts are jammed, and our family therapists are swamped. Our elementary schools are Ritalin-controlled; our high schools are installing metal detectors and security cameras and hiring armed guards; and our college campuses are soaked in armed guards. It's time for solutions. But how can we find solutions when today's teens seem so distant? Let's look at a couple of stories.

CASE STUDY

Matt grumpily opened one eye, slammed his alarm off, and pulled the covers over his head. Every muscle in his body ached from the previous night's wrestling match. He had won, but he'd paid a heavy price for the victory: in addition to sore muscles, he suffered a massive mat burn on his elbow and a sprained right ankle.

"Come on, Matt. Get up," John, Matt's older brother, called from their bathroom. "You aren't making me late again today."

Matt rolled his eyes. For half a second, he considered convincing his mom to call him in sick, but he quickly remembered his math test in third period. Mustering every ounce of energy possible for a seventeen-year-old at six in the morning, Matt threw the covers aside and swung his legs onto the floor.

Forty-five minutes and two arguments later, Matt and John slumped into John's car and headed for school. John picked up right where the second argument had left off—questioning Matt about "the latest" girl he had been seeing.

"Look, Matt," John said, "all I'm saying is that I've heard she's slept around a lot. Just know what you're getting yourself into."

"Whatever, John," Matt retorted with a sneer. "Like you have any room to talk. And what do you care if she's slept around? Stay out of my business."

"Just know what you are getting yourself into. And don't come crying to me later."

"Yeah, whatever," Matt said, tuning the radio to his favorite station.

"You act like you're invincible or something. You think you can get away with whatever you want to do," John said as he changed the station back to its usual spot.

"What are you talking about?"

"You know exactly what I'm talking about. You sleep around all the time, you drink too much every weekend, you smoke weed before every wrestling match . . . aren't you at least worried about getting caught?"

John continued, but Matt felt he had heard enough, and he tuned his brother out. Matt had been listening to John preach to him for months, and he was sick of it. Ever since John started going to church with a girl he knew, he had been berating Matt about his "lifestyle." John's life hadn't even changed all that much—he still partied most weekends—but Matt had to admit that John's perspective on a lot of things was changing.

Still, Matt didn't want to be bothered with it. He was young. He wanted to have fun. He wanted to be carefree. Wasn't that the life every young kid should have?

CASE STUDY

Jessica's mom handed her a list of reminders, blew her a kiss, grabbed the laptop, and rushed out the door. By the time Jessica looked up to wave good-bye, her mom was gone.

She looked down at the list in her hand: "Pick up your sister at 3. Drop off dry cleaning. Heat up macaroni casserole for dinner."

Jessica sighed. She desperately wanted to go out with her friends that night, but she knew it wouldn't happen. As usual, her mom would be later than originally planned, and she'd have to entertain her kid sister for hours.

At least she could escape at school for most of the day. She'd probably skip fourth hour and get high with her friends at Darren's house. Two month's ago, Jessica had smoked pot for the first time at a party; now, she got stoned almost every day. Like everyone else she knew, Jessica and her friends had discovered it, enjoyed it, and made it a way of life.

But then, high school was like that. You had more independence and, in most afternoons, less to do. Alcohol was cool for a while, but it was smelly, expensive, and hard to get. Marijuana was everywhere, and it was easier to cover up.

Sex was another issue. Jessica smiled as she thought about all the boys she had turned down at countless parties. The thought of sex was still repulsive to her. Most of her friends had lost their virginity over the last couple of years, but Jessica was proud of herself for "holding out." She wanted to wait for the right guy to come along. Her mom had told her to wait until marriage (though her mom hadn't followed that advice herself), and Jessica thought that was a pretty good plan. But she also knew that if she fell in love with the right person she'd be ready. Her mom was out of touch, anyway. Old school.

More or less, Jessica felt as though she were a pretty normal high school girl. She did her schoolwork, partied with friends, experimented with drugs and alcohol, and tried to keep everything straight. She knew high school was only a stepping-stone until college, and she wanted to have fun while she could. Her mom was never around, and she hadn't seen her dad in years, but she felt like she was taking pretty good care of herself.

CASE STUDY

The two young men entered the normal-looking high school on a normal-looking day. Students much like Matt, John, and Jessica milled about with friends and teachers, virtually ignoring the two guys as they stormed defiantly into the school. The two young men had something on their minds, but no one seemed to notice.

Until the first shots rang out.

In seconds, Columbine High School in Littleton, Colorado, was transformed from a building full of typical high school teenagers dealing with typical high school issues to a battleground of horrific warfare.

April 20 is no longer remembered merely as the birthday of the tyrant Adolf Hitler. It is now marked as one of the most sorrowful days in recent American history. It is the day that Eric Harris and Dylan Klebold took a distorted notion of justice into their own hands and killed twelve of their classmates and a teacher before taking their own lives. That morning, the two seventeen-year-olds walked into their school with four guns and over thirty pipe bombs and executed a rampage they had been planning for over a year.

The shooting began outside during the 11:30 lunch hour. Hundreds of students in the cafeteria stared in confusion toward the sound of gunfire and bombs, trying to determine if they were the brunt of some odd senior prank. Several friends and classmates had remembered two boys making a "movie" for class about killing jocks, and for a moment they wondered, and hoped, that the two teens entering the cafeteria in masks and trench coats were playing a joke. But as real bullets and shrapnel began slicing into the bodies of their friends, they realized that this was no joke. In a horrific moment, these students were faced with the grim reality of death and destruction at the hands of their classmates.

After killing several students execution-style in the cafeteria, Eric and Dylan worked their way to the library, spraying bullets, tossing bombs, and cackling with laughter. Students ducked behind stairwells, barricaded themselves in classrooms and closets, climbed into the ceiling, and slithered along the ground to save their lives. Some ducked down and pulled out cell phones, alerting the police and their parents. Some scribbled quick notes to friends and family, wanting to say "I love you" one last time. Others hid under tables, praying silently that the sounds of screams and gunfire would cease. "[Eric and Dylan] were shooting everywhere," said Nick Foss, a senior at Columbine. "I've never been so frightened in my life."[1]

The terror ended twenty minutes later in the library. There, Eric and Dylan handpicked a few more students to execute—students whose names are familiar to us all now, such as Isaiah Shoels, who was killed simply because of the color of his skin, and Cassie Bernall, whose confession of faith in God cost her life. Soon, in an ironic act of mercy, the two teens aimed their guns at themselves and ended the massacre. With teens weeping, halls riddled with bullets and blood, and a nation anxiously watching, the crime was finally over, but the terror had only begun.

Shock, tears, and prayers were the immediate response, followed by a loss of simple innocence: security systems, metal detectors, armed teachers, and paranoia are the legacy of Columbine. For the two of us, April 20 seemed to move forward in slow motion as we worked frantically to take care of the many families in our church who were being impacted by the events happening only fifty miles from our front door. Within hours, our telephones began to ring off the hook with the inevitable speculations and desperate questions about the two boys: Were they abused as children? Were their dads too busy? Did they attend church? What about my own kids? Should I pull my child out of public school? What has our country come to? What's next? Where have we gone wrong?

Good questions. And they deserve good answers.

So Where Are the Answers?

As we read and reread the tragic headlines in our newspapers and magazines, we see the message. As we watch the divorce rate in America soar, it becomes clear to us. As we hear the heartbreaking stories of families suffering under the tyranny of bad decisions, reality glares us in the face: something's wrong with our kids—something deeper than simply "good kids gone bad." Numb to violence, desperate for attention, bound by bad habits, our teenagers are in trouble. It's like there's a tornado violently sucking our kids into destruction. Our kids are caught in a fight for survival. They're trapped in a violent downward spiral, and we've got to do something about it.

But the answers may not be found in the places where we've been looking. Psychologists, sociologists, doctors, and pastors have been searching desperately for the answers to the problems teenagers face. Countless tests, studies, and experiments have been done, and while many of their conclusions contain elements of truth, their answers seem incomplete: "Understand that these kids are basically good"; "Let them become who they are"; "Let them express themselves."

The truth is, these answers alone are not producing healthy families and good kids. They sound fine in a clinical setting or in a book, but they don't work well enough in practice. Our grandparents seemed to understand child care and family dynamics better than many of the experts of our generation. Farms, extended families, and connected communities embraced a set of values and produced a strength of character that we are struggling to duplicate in our world of cell phones, compacted appointment schedules, and fast food.

But our realities prevail. We all like many of the opportunities of our modern culture, so we've got to learn how to produce good children in the midst of movement. We can't slow down, and we don't want to go back. We're going forward while working overtime to help our kids avoid the pitfalls, and our work is cut out for us. The pressures all of our families face are more fierce, the walls of safety are weaker, and resisting negative trends in our society often seems futile. Today, raising teenagers is a lot more like negotiating with an alien race in a *Star Trek* episode than helping an adolescent navigate through the tough teenage years.

Indeed, we face tough questions every day:

- How can I talk to my teenager without getting frustrated?
- How do I raise my kids without their father around the house?
- Why can't I get "into" their brain?
- Where's the line between parent and friend?

The questions go on and on and on. Frustration sets in and tempers flare. The next thing you know, Mom's slumped over the kitchen sink weeping at the idea of losing her kids, and the drama continues to unfold. . . .

Hold it. Stop. Pause. There is hope. Parents can be confident, and teenagers can be exceptional. One of us, John, is a youth minister who works with a thousand teenagers every week. The other, Ted, is a senior minister who coaches thousands of adults and their families from week to week. As we work every day with families, some successful and vibrant, and others broken and desperate, we find that there is a road map to successful parenting. It can happen, but it doesn't happen naturally. The secrets of success are seen clearly when we examine the habits of families that really work. Lately, though, it seems as though the road map has been crumpled by a flurry of images and differing opinions. The recent events in our society point us toward the need to recalibrate a successful path for our kids.

COLUMBINE HITS HOME

The afternoon of the Columbine tragedy is one John won't soon forget:

> I had been working frantically that day looking for a couple of illustrations for an upcoming sermon. I was moving through our youth office in my let's-get-to-work-people manner. As I passed by the TV monitor in our video editor's office bay, I noticed a clump of youth workers gathered around the screen.
>
> "What's the deal?" I asked.
>
> "It's a school shooting," came the reply.
>
> "How many does that make now, nine?" I asked carelessly as I walked past, still focused on my own goals and not realizing the gravity of what was actually happening. But within minutes I began to understand that what was unraveling at Columbine High School—just an hour's drive from my house—was different from the other school shootings. With our radios and TVs tuned to the news, we listened and prayed as the day crept on. . . .
>
> Later that same day, a woman in her thirties (I'll call her Sandy) walked through my office door and slumped into a chair. "I'm losing my son," she said. After twenty minutes with this desperate mom, I grasped the seriousness of her situation. Knowing that Ted was only a few doors away, I called to see if he was available for an emergency appointment. To my surprise, he walked into the office a few min-

utes later. For the next forty-five minutes, we listened to one of the saddest accounts of adolescence we had ever heard. I listened as Pastor Ted gave frank, honest advice to the distressed mother. After setting up an intervention plan and bringing the discussion to a stopping place, we escorted Sandy out of the building. As she drove away, we glanced at each other in the foyer of our church, both realizing the weight of our responsibility to parents.

As the events were unfolding in Littleton a mere fifty miles away from us, a loving mother was acutely reminded of her struggles with her own son. For years, Sandy had been trying desperately to get answers to her questions. Her story is not singular. And her son is not alone. There are hundreds of kids just as lonely, frustrated, and hurting as Eric Harris and Dylan Klebold, and just as many moms as desperate as Sandy. And they're hoping someone will hear their cries and heal their pain.

THE UNAVOIDABLE PLEA

In the lonely countryside of East Germany there is a sleepy rural village that has been isolated from the rest of the world for nearly five hundred years. It was isolated, that is, until the summer of 1944.

In that small village, a single church served the entire town. The church sat on a tiny plot of land right next to the village's only connection to the rest of the world—the railroad tracks. Every Sunday during the morning worship service, a train filled with coal or timber would chug down the tracks next to the church. Outside of the minor distraction of the clanking wheels, no one in the town ever thought anything of it.

But by the summer of 1944, World War II had changed much of the world. During that summer, at precisely 11:14 A.M. every Sunday, the same train would pass by that little German church. Now, however, the train was no longer filled with coal or timber but with thousands of German Jews. As the train would pass by, the sound of passengers screaming would fill the church walls. Each Sunday, the townspeople could clearly hear the terrible anguish of genocide outside their doors.

The small town was so shaken by the horror of the train and its innocent passengers that people began to complain of the noise . . . and feel the inevitable guilt. They must have known that they were not to blame for the crisis of the Jews, but they could not escape a sense of shame for what was happening to them. Quickly, a solution was offered: every Sunday at precisely 11:10 A.M., the church organist would belt out a hymn so rich and so strong that the members of the little church couldn't help but sing along. The sweet melody of age-old hymns would rise from the little church, rolling over hills and valleys, drowning the sound of the people crying out for help just a few feet away.

It was the hope of the townspeople that the music would drown out the sounds of the sorrow of the Jews—if not in reality, then at least, for God's sake, in their own consciences.

We are that little church. And without a doubt, voices are coming to us from families in the train. Slasher movies, MTV, chiseled bodies on *Baywatch,* and sexually seductive cultural heroes are pressing our families to the breaking point. The demonstration of wholesome lives, kind deeds, and long-lasting relationships is disappearing. The sounds of a young generation and their parents can be heard everywhere: on TV, in magazines, music, in the headlines of our newspapers, and in the hallways of our schools. If we prick our ears just a little, we can plainly hear their plea for help.

This book is the result of a rude awakening, combined with the culmination of years of hearing the sounds, the voices, the calls for help. For us, the tragedy at Columbine High School was the catalyst that jolted us into further action. After years of working with families on the front lines of everyday life, we simply couldn't ignore the voice of Columbine. But it isn't the only voice. There are hundreds, no, thousands of voices. Columbine just happened to raise its volume over the clamor of the rest.

In the upcoming chapters, we'll discuss with you how to confidently raise strong young men and women. But first, let's take a look at what happens to create the intense downward spiral in teens' lives and what we as parents can do to stop it.

CHAPTER

Two

Breaking the
Downward Spiral

Trouble is, kids feel they have to shock their elders, and each generation grows into something harder to shock.

BEN LINDSEY

What makes a teenager a teenager? This is a question of much debate between parents, physicians, sociologists, psychologists, educators, and geneticists. While all experts agree that human development is very complex, they also agree that parental influence is the single most powerful external factor in a teenager's life. As parents, we have the ultimate opportunity to influence the mental, emotional, and spiritual makeup of our children. We can help shape the values that determine their choices, priorities, and desires, and encourage them to develop a healthy life perspective. As parents, it is up to us to teach our children what it means to be alive.

Knowing this, parents attempt to insure a strong education for their children, expose them to positive role models, build a moral fabric into their lives, and provide for them financially. But in spite of good intentions, many kids still go astray. Week after week, parents come into our offices saying, "I've done everything I know to do. I've loved my children. I've always encouraged them and been there for them. But they're still rebelling." Kids can be raised in a healthy family and have a strong community of faith and an abundance of safe and wholesome fun, but for some reason, the downward spiral that every parent dreads can still begin.

The good news is that the spiral, once begun, can be broken. We regularly see families break the cycle of turmoil. How do they do it? By learning how to respond correctly to conflict. Raising a teenager requires a strong ability to manage conflict. Conventional wisdom says that conflict should be avoided, but, when parenting, conflict is inevitable and necessary. Conflict begins the night the baby comes home from the hospital, when the initial battle over "who's in charge here" takes place. These little struggles are important and should not be avoided outright—each one is an opportunity to establish roles and affirm relationships. Of course, as our children become teenagers, the conflicts become more severe (take heart, parents: these conflicts are usually resolved as our babies grow into their forties!), which means it is all the more imperative that we learn to respond wisely. The way we manage conflict can mean the difference between a teen who crashes into despair and a teen who breaks out of the downward spiral.

Throughout the balance of this book, we will address specific ways to protect our children and respond to various areas of conflict. But to respond effectively, we need to be able to understand the five stages in the downward spiral, a process that begins with a breakdown in communication and can ultimately lead to a broken teenager:

- *Strained Communication:* Negative response to parents
- *Testing Independence:* As input is assimilated, the teen's "new self" emerges
- *New Friends:* Teens begin to define themselves by their associations
- *New Standards:* Habits, standards, and view of life are redefined
- *Consequences:* The results of the teen's responses become evident

STRAINED COMMUNICATION

The first stage in the downward spiral of a teenager is a break-down in communication. This breakdown usually begins in a quiet corner of the home: a "you don't understand me" argument in the kitchen, a misread glance at the dinner table, repeated nights of soli-tude in the bedroom. Usually benign at first, miscommunication will grow and fester if it is not addressed. A simple misunder-standing can evolve into a venomous exchange of words, a door angrily slammed, or a week without words. For some families the breakdown is not that extreme. For others it's much worse. In any case, if the communication in a household is poor, the door swings wide open for a host of problems to be welcomed inside.

Strained communication is always the unintended consequence of poorly choosing our actions or words. A harsh word or broken promise can produce unexpected grief, so we must be respectful in our actions and deliberate in our communication. It's like pouring milk on Corn Flakes (stick with us for a second). When you pour milk onto a bowl of Corn Flakes, if the milk hits one of the curled flakes, the milk will fly out of the bowl onto your shirt, pants, table, or the guy sitting next to you. When pouring milk on Corn Flakes, you really want the milk in the bowl so you can eat your Corn Flakes, but if you accidentally pour it on the wrong flake, it ends up in the wrong place.

Like spilled milk, strained family communication is an unin-tended consequence of careless actions and words. No one says, "When I grow up I want to be an alcoholic and ruin my family." No one plans on spending a life in prison. But if we aren't careful, poor choices will take us places we don't want to go. To avoid unin-tended consequences, we must anticipate what we're building. Too often we say something reckless without realizing that our words are seeds that can grow into bitter hatred. Too often we do some-thing careless without realizing that our actions are the first steps on a long road of internal conflict. Are we thinking, saying, and doing things that will produce benefits, or are we inadvertently sowing the seeds of our own destruction? Knowing what our words and actions may produce means everything.

The art of successful living is not merely reducing the number of negative incidents and pain in our lives; it is properly responding to those incidents and pain. Faulty communication starts when someone feels rejected or betrayed, and it can usually be healed immediately. But sometimes the problem isn't detected until we've produced a reaction of silence or hostility that is the unintended consequence of missing a baseball game, being too busy to follow through with a promised camping trip, snapping at someone over dinner.

Inevitably, some baseball games will be missed, some camping trips will be canceled, and small outbursts occur from time to time, but we've got to avoid prolonged miscommunication as a result of those disappointments. Fortunately, the answer is simple: spend time with your kids and talk with them. Create a safe environment for great conversations. Take a walk. Grab a soda together. Go into your teenager's room and lay on the floor until they start talking. Take a trip together without the cell phone and laptop. Protect the family dinnertime or breakfast time. Drive them to school instead of sending them on the bus or letting them walk. Meet them for lunch or take them to breakfast. Go hang out at their favorite place with them. Let them come into your room late at night or early in the morning just to talk and laugh. Do what it takes to find out what they are really thinking. Give your teen an opportunity to connect with you. If you were wrong about something, sincerely apologize. If they were wrong, coach them. But don't let silent wounds define your relationship.

Remember that open communication is only possible in an atmosphere of love, trust, and integrity. All of us connect with others because of love—a desire to live for another person's good. In a loving atmosphere, people connect with one another naturally, thus making one another's lives better. Constructive communication can develop and grow through the adolescent years, but never if our relationships are clouded with deception, betrayal, or selfishness. To avoid this, develop character. Build relationships with trust and integrity. Discover the strength of family and surround your family with strong heartfelt relationships that connect people for a lifetime of security and strength. As Eleanor Roosevelt said, "Character building begins in infancy, and continues until death." If our relationships with our kids are rooted in love and trust, we will provide them an atmosphere to communicate constructively, helping them develop into exceptional teens. But without love, it's every man for himself, with yelling, defensiveness, hurt, and pain. In this atmosphere, when communication gets strained, we won't succumb to the temptation to assume that the problem will take care of itself. Loving environments don't allow us to say, "It'll soon be over. No need to sweat it. I'll talk to them tomorrow." Instead, they fix the problems because they know that tomorrow comes too late. At all costs, we must build lives that avoid just staying afloat in the ocean of troubled adolescence.

Testing Independence

In the teen years, our children go through the incredible journey from *dependence* through *independence* toward *interdependence*. Dependence, which usually lasts from newborn through eleven or twelve years old, is when children depend completely upon others to care for them. About the time they are entering puberty, their desire for independence is taking shape. Their bodies are bigger, their ideas are substantive, and even though they love their parents, they begin to develop an identity apart from home. As they are able to drive the car, decide what clothes to wear, and choose which classes to take, they begin defining themselves. This usually lasts from the age of thirteen to the late teens or early twenties. It is during the years of independence that so many parents and teens struggle as the teens begin to gain personal responsibility and increased autonomy; it is important to note that independence is not the same as rebellion, which is the teen's trying to establish his or her own authority in hostile resistance against others.

As we coach teens through adolescence, a wise balance of listening and speaking, staying connected and letting go, and leading our teens to wisely choose others to influence them—such as teachers, the parents of their friends, pastors, and others in the community—is a major step in their growing through independence toward interdependence. When we lead them wisely through this process, our teens never have to separate from their family to find their individuality.

The process of our children clarifying their own identity can be a wonderful time for teens and their families, even though the inevitable difficulties will arise. Adolescence can be both intriguing and rewarding for parents as we see our teens broadening their intellectual and emotional reach. We all grow when our teens begin to articulate their own thoughts about the world, society, and people. Watching our kids play ball, sing in a choir, pass a difficult course, or play an instrument is remarkably gratifying.

Since these are the years when our kids begin to be valued by their own friends, teachers, and members of the community, parents have the satisfaction of knowing that years of parenting are providing tangible results. We don't want to imply that adolescence is all roses, but we do want to strongly emphasize that adolescence has many elements that can bring great delight to a family—if we'll understand how to lead in wisdom.

Our role as parents is to lead our kids through these stages so they can become responsible adults. If we manage conflicts well and keep the lines of communication open, encouraging our teenagers through independence can be an exciting process that will produce results. Poor communication, though, will inhibit our ability to lead through this stage, and our young people might easily spiral into stubbornness and resentment. If there isn't frequent healthy communication, we find ourselves running to work or other activities to avoid parenting our kids. Why? Maybe to avoid the conflict. Maybe to ignore the consequences. Maybe because we're scared to death.

Letters like the following appear on our desks all the time:

Dear *Anyone Who Can Help,*

My name is Alice. I feel like I am losing my daughter, and I need your guidance. I could write pages about the last few months, but I'll start with the other morning, when I happened to walk downstairs in time to see her pop a pill into her mouth. I sighed to myself and acted naïve. "Are you taking vitamins for track, Beth?" I asked. Surprised to hear my voice that early, she swung around in her chair. "Oh, hi, Mom. Umm. Yeah, I just grabbed a Vitamin C. I can feel a cold coming on." "Well, that should do the trick, then," I said.

I knew Beth had been on birth control for the past six months, but I wasn't about to say anything about it. I was worried, but I couldn't afford to do anything stupid and lose her right now. Not in the middle of changing jobs. And after all, I wasn't any different when I was 15.

But it wasn't until I sat down for my coffee that it really all began.

"Mom, I'm thinking about getting a tattoo."

Even as I'm writing this letter I can't quite put my finger on what happened next. I just snapped. The tattoo wasn't that big a deal—it was just that everything was piling up. The pills. The late nights. The distance she puts between us. Her new friends. Her hair—or lack of it—and on and on. Within seconds, our kitchen was transformed into a hurricane of voices and anger. We both said things we didn't mean. Before I knew it, Beth was storming out the door. She was about to slam it behind her when she turned to me and yelled, "No wonder Dad left. I don't blame him. I can't breathe in this house!" Then she left. And that's when the tears came.

Honestly, I don't know where I went wrong. I've done everything I know to do. What's happening to my daughter? What happened to my little girl? Please help me.

Sincerely,
A mother in trouble

Undoubtedly it is difficult to walk teens through the years when they are trying to make decisions for themselves. These conflicts are uncomfortable and foreign. But we must be willing to find a solution, for it's during these turbulent years of life that teens need us most, and want us most. Rest assured: they'd never tell us that. Actually, they'll probably say just the opposite and with just the right expletives to convince us to leave them alone. But they don't really mean it. Don't believe them. Use wisdom, but keep pressing on.

As parents, the temptation during the independence stage is to over-befriend our teens. While friendship is important, our primary role is parent, not pal. Certainly, our kids need to know that we love them. They need for us to talk to them, to wisely enforce values and to play with them. But you are the standard maker, the rule maker, and, yes, sometimes the matchmaker. Teens want a benchmark in their lives, and you're it. When our teens begin to try out their wings of independence, sometimes we react like a pendulum. One minute, we walk on eggshells around them, not wanting to offend them as we, usually unsuccessfully, try to coax them to listen to us. The next minute we try to bring down the hammer. The problem is, we usually do this too late and our wonderful teens end up responding with not-so-wonderful words.

New Friends

All of us are preprogrammed to be successful in groups—we're drawn to each other. We need other people to be happy and healthy. And what is true for us is also true for teens. As we begin to see our teens assert their independence, we begin to wonder how and why they suddenly changed. At this time, teens are going through an affiliation stage. During this process, teenagers experiment with whom they want to model themselves after and whom they want to be liked by. Affiliation comes in all kinds of shapes, sizes, and forms. It is represented in sports, hobbies, clubs, church, and clothes.

If communication can stay healthy and open during this process, usually teens will be attracted to friends and organizations that line up with your family's "mission statement." A mission statement, which we'll discuss in detail in the next chapter, is the guiding statement of purpose for your family. If you communicate this purpose to your teens and guide them successfully through independence, the things that make mom and dad tick will be the things that motivate the teenager. If not, the teen will affiliate with organizations and people that make them feel accepted or pique their interests. This is when teens fall into the traps of gangs, hate clubs, and other negative influences. As a young person begins to associate with new friends, the habits and standards of those friends will become the basis for a new mentality within that teen.

You have likely heard the words, "Mom, don't judge my friends. You don't know them!" It's the classic good-teen-gone-bad, good-parent-gone-mad situation. As the saying goes, "Show me your friends and I'll show you you're future." There's another similar proverb: "Bad company corrupts good character." We must help our kids realize the importance of choosing friends wisely. As you read this, you might think, "But who am I to determine who my child decides to embrace as friends?" Well, you are their parent. It's okay for you to help them decide whom they should befriend, and even correct their poor decisions.

NEW STANDARDS

With communication gone, the thrill of independence discovered, and new friends to spend time with, it is only a matter of time before a teen develops a new set of standards. In this stage, old family values are challenged as archaic and irrelevant, or at least escapable, while alternate standards seem exciting, trendy, and easy to embrace. In very little time, a teen's values can change dramatically. John can remember a meeting he had with a parent whose teen was undergoing a shift in life standards:

> I was on my way out the door for a much-needed vaca-
> tion when my phone rang. I fought the temptation to keep
> walking and turned around to pick up the receiver. Between
> sobs on the other end, I could make out the desperate

sounds of a mother's voice. "Meet me in my office in twenty minutes," I said. An hour later, I had heard enough for a month's worth of counseling appointments. For sixty minutes, this mom told me the story of her daughter, Cathy. She told me how only three years ago, Cathy was a bright, happy girl who was excited about school and eager to become a nurse. Now this content little twelve-year-old girl had transformed, seemingly overnight, into a reclusive, rebellious, brazen fifteen-year-old "Goth." Pigtails, ribbons, and bloomers had been replaced with spiked green hair, size-forty-two jeans, and a tongue bar. Cathy was once happy to walk through the mall hand-in-hand with her mother testing the perfume at all the big stores, but now she insisted on hanging out with her friends and holding cigarettes between her black painted fingernails.

As I sat and listened to the tragic tale, I realized that the jeans, makeup, and hair weren't the issue. It went much deeper than that. The people who had embraced her had unwittingly formed her decisions, habits, and new worldview. As the rule goes, whoever loves the most, wins. Actually, whoever is perceived to love the most wins. The acceptance and appreciation that was found in Cathy's new friends helped her to establish an identity of her own. The attitudes, habits, and convictions of her new group quickly became her accepted culture. The music, styles, and tastes of her new affiliations had trumped the connection to her family.

Many parents have watched this exact thing happen to their teen. In what seems like a few days, a teenager can change from "All-American" to "America's Most Wanted." Ironically, most of these teens never would have guessed that they would ever join up with that crowd. But once the downward spiral begins, it becomes a natural progression.

In Alaska, there is a legend of a unique method of hunting the feared timber wolves without actually hunting them at all. As the story goes, the Eskimo wolf hunters dip a knife in the fresh blood of an animal and allow it to dry on the blade of the knife. The hunters continue to do this over and over until the blade is nothing more than a mass of dried blood. Then the hunters trek into the wilderness, place the knife upside down into the snow, and go home. During the late hours of the night, the scent of blood travels over the dark woods to the carnivores. Instinctively, they find the knife and begin to lick the blood from the blade. The blood drives the wolves into a frenzy and they continue to devour it until only the shiny blade remains. As they cut their own tongues on the knife, they fail to realize that now it's their own blood that they're devouring. In the morning, the Eskimo wolf hunters find the bodies of the wolves laying next to the blade, killed from bleeding to death.

Over time, the temptations of life become alluring to our kids. Unless we put a stop to it, the temptations become irresistible. It's our job to rescue our kids. The truth is, we'd love to make it the responsibility of everyone around us—the school, the church, the counselors, Hollywood. But they can't do it like we can. Ultimately, it's up to us.

Wait. Don't drop this book and go get a drink. The good news is that you can make it. You can help change the course of your teenager's life. That's the value of parents.

CONSEQUENCES

As our sons and daughters progress down the spiral, we soon find them suffering under the consequences of their decisions. Again, we can intervene at any stage in this process if we are aware and thoughtful and can reestablish communication with our children. But if communication is allowed to falter and they become stubborn and independent, choosing wrong friends, and beginning to live according to their own rules and standards, poor decisions will begin to produce destructive consequences. Unfortunately, these consequences are sometimes permanent, which is why this book is so important. Our goal is to build families that can lead teens through difficult years into positive interdependence with others. If that goal is not achieved, though, the consequences of the downward spiral will appear in one or more of these areas: mental, social, spiritual, or physical.

- *Mental Consequences:* Teens exhibiting mental consequences of the downward spiral seem to have "checked out" of life. Blank stares, few words, hollow emotions, and preoccupation with mind-numbing activities often characterize this mental suicide.
- *Social Consequences:* "I don't care what you think about me any-more!" Such is the attitude that saturates a teen sliding down the spiral. Here, the "bad boy" attitude starts to take over as teens stop caring about any positive social dynamics or constraints.
- *Spiritual Consequences:* "I hope I go to hell. That's where the parties are going to be anyway. All my friends will be there!" This is the consequence of our teens believing that there is no God, no set of divine moral standards, and no concern for eternal judgment. This consequence accompanies a lack of respect for life, the civil rights of others, or personal responsibility.
- *Physical Consequences:* As we all know, teens can take out the consequences of their downward spiral on themselves:

"Erica" walked shyly up to the front of our youth chapel one night after a youth meeting. She stood patiently in line behind several others, who were asking questions ranging from, "How do I tell my dad I'm pregnant?" to "How do you know when you're in love?" But Erica had a hollow gaze to go with her tragic story. The state had taken her from her mom at eleven. Her dad was thrown into prison for murder when she was nine. For five years, she'd been juggled back and forth between foster homes. She'd drowned her frustration in drugs, alcohol, and sex.

Then came the clincher. With tearstained eyes, she exposed her arms. Obvious slash marks were a testament to her inward pain. The consequences of bad decisions by her dad were finally being realized. A little girl had tried to take her life because she felt as though it were already gone.

Obviously, we have our work cut out for us as parents. The good news is that we can make it. Spotting the signs of downward spiral is the first step to stopping the fall. Once you've identified the warning signs, it's time to build strength into your family that will keep spirits high, elevate trust, and increase the purpose of the home. Now we're getting to the good part. In the next eight chapters, we'll first discuss how to shape your teen's purpose, mind, character, and personality, and then examine four external collateral strengths—family, government authority, school, and faith—you can use as tools to weather the teenage storm and move into smooth sailing.

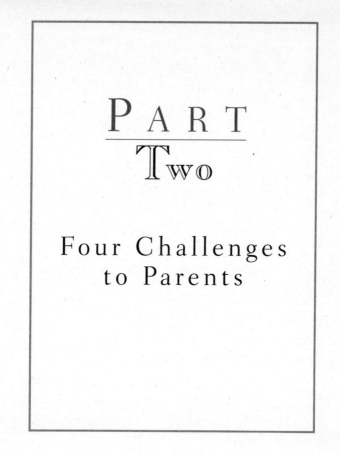

PART
Two

Four Challenges
to Parents

CHAPTER
Three

Mold Their Purpose: The Passport to Great Lives

It is not possible for civilization to flow backwards while there is youth in the world.

HELEN KELLER

Star Wars: Episode One: The Phantom Menace was the promotional bonanza of the past decade. Prior to its opening on May 19, 1999, thousands of people camped outside movie theaters to purchase tickets and see the premiere. In the weeks beforehand, couples dressed in *Star Wars* garb were married in ticket lines, Europeans flew to the United States to get in line for tickets, and whole Web sites were dedicated to counting down the hours, minutes, and seconds until the premiere. *Star Wars* characters graced the cover of seemingly every major magazine in North America. For *Star Wars* fanatics, this was all in good fun, a chance to revel in their favorite hobby for all the world to see. But for millions of more passive moviegoers, the *Star Wars* hype begged the question "Why?"

The reason for the success of *Star Wars* is simple: its story resonates deeply with people. Sure, it has the brilliant special effects of George Lucas and his team, but more importantly, it is a story that has captured the imagination of two generations. *Star Wars* is about a hero, a team, a villain, a family. In short, it is about people with purpose. All the characters in the series have that special gleam in their eye, that decided impetus in their gait, that direct tone in their voices that says, "I am *about* something." It is this quality, the quality of purpose, that makes *Star Wars* so attractive.

Star Wars isn't the only example; in fact, it is the least of the examples. Historically, we have always rallied around people who have purpose, for better or for worse. Moses. Mohammed. Jesus Christ. Martin Luther King Jr. Sojourner Truth. George Washington. Gandhi. Mother Teresa. Those and hundreds like them unified masses of people with their world-changing purposes. And even people who had much lower, evil pursuits, such as Adolf Hitler and Joseph Stalin, were able to accomplish their goals because they tapped into that most common of human desires: the desire for purpose.

Why is purpose so important to us? Because it establishes us. Purpose tells us who we are. But it doesn't just answer the big questions, such as "Why are we alive?" Purpose answers every "why" in our lives. And every one of us, at one time or another, has to ask "Why?" Why do we drive the speed limit? Why do we save for retirement? Why do we work hard? Why are we trying to raise great teens?

People who find purpose find an answer. People who don't develop a fragile constitution that can't sustain a healthy self-esteem, resulting in profound feelings of loneliness, sadness, and lack of direction. With a clear purpose the answers to questions about how we should spend our money, treat our spouses, think about God, and, of course, raise our children, become painstakingly clear. With purpose clearly defined, life is less of a dilemma and more of a focused, proactive exercise of living out the things we believe in. Purpose causes us to do substantive things with our lives. Without it, we become drones in the beehive of life, just one of the millions waiting to die. But with purpose, we reach further, stretch higher, try longer, and achieve more.

THE LACK OF PURPOSE IN TEENS

We sometimes go to Denny's for hot fudge sundaes after late-night meetings. These excursions aren't passive relaxation—they are quests: quests for fudge, maraschino cherries, and nuts; quests for vanilla, chocolate, and strawberry; quests for ten minutes of sweet delight, followed by thirty minutes of aching stomachs. Recently, after a particularly long day, we stormed into Denny's with little but this quest, this *purpose,* if you will, on our minds. As we sat devouring our ice cream and talking about weekend plans, we noticed four rough-looking teenagers sitting in a booth across the room. We looked at each other as if to say, "I dare you." Needless to say, we both got up from the table and slowly began our trek across Denny's.

As we approached the table, we made a quick assessment of the teens. One, a girl of fifteen or sixteen, was slumped down in the booth. Her eyes were glazed, and it was obvious that she was there to sober up after what had probably been a pretty exciting night for her. She was wearing a black leather jacket with an anarchy symbol scrawled on the front pocket. Next to her was a slightly older boy with a cigarette pinched tightly in his fingers; he kept leaning over the table with vivid expressions, making gestures at the policeman standing by the door of the restaurant. The other two teens, a boy and a girl, were sitting together talking and kissing as though their friends weren't even there. The boy had purple hair and a tattoo around his neck. The girl had two rings on her right eyebrow and a chain connecting a ring on her ear with a ring on her lip.

Our hearts beat faster as we neared the table, knowing that they were likely to laugh us off. We asked the teens if they could talk with us for a while, and they motioned for us to sit down. After the formalities and a little small talk, we discovered a familiar scenario. All four teenagers had parents who were professionals. Each of their parents had time to enjoy six-figure incomes but no time to raise kids. The lumps in our throats grew as the teens openly told their stories—stories of big dreams and desperate hopes. One wanted to become a zoologist, another a surgeon, another a computer programmer, and another an entrepreneur. They all had big dreams, but they were lacking something—a sense of purpose, a sense that they could actually accomplish any of those things, a belief that there was any real reason they should pursue the dreams in the first place. Their dreams were big, but they were empty. No one had given them a reason to chase their goals, and the teens were dying inside because of it.

In many ways, the problems with kids today, from Eric and Dylan at Columbine to the fourteen-year-old boy searching for pornography on the Internet, can be linked to a lack of purpose. The Book of Proverbs says, "Without purpose, people perish." All teenagers have dreams, but many lack a sense of purpose to guide those dreams and help them take action. Eric Harris was pursuing a career in the Marines until the week before the shootings, but he lacked that special impetus that would have directed him toward better choices after the Marines turned him down.

Purpose is the thing that connects a distant dream with the reality that it can be attained. Purpose ignites passion in us for achievement. Without purpose, our lives are reduced to nothing more than a sad melody of halfhearted platitudes: "I hope so," "Maybe one day," "If I try hard enough." Purpose is fiery; it is saying "I know I will" rather than "I think I can." Purpose is living a life bigger than yourself.

In John Irving's famous novel, *A Prayer for Owen Meany,* the title character, an odd midget who, for most of the book, is a disgruntled teenager, discovers early in life that he is alive for one special purpose. Though he doesn't know exactly what that purpose is, he firmly believes that he has a unique destiny. Owen Meany's friends and family all disapprove of his irrational beliefs; they'd be much more comfortable if he'd just "go with the flow" and make decisions based on circumstance, such as his physical limitations, not on a higher purpose. But Owen is resolute; he knows God created him for a particular mission, and he makes choices according to that mission, not according to his whim, physical stature, or peer pressure. By the book's end, Owen has faced every battle and come out a champion, his purposed fulfilled, his destiny complete.

When real purpose gets into a teenager, no force in the world can stop the upward spiral. Like a determined marathon runner, purpose gives teens the strength to put one foot in front of the other in spite of what their body is telling them. Purpose is the motivation behind every truly great leader. With purpose, a teenager will flourish. With purpose, there is an intense value attached to every decision a teenager makes.

For instance, let's say that a young man has made the decision that he is to become the United States Ambassador to France (notice that he isn't simply *dreaming* of being Ambassador: he has determined that he *is going to be* Ambassador). As this young man grows up and goes through the normal situations that all teens go through, he can begin to make decisions according to his purpose, not his situation. Let's say he goes to a party some Friday night. Everyone's taking drugs and his friends want him to join in. Now remember, he has in him a sense of who he will become—the Ambassador to France. He may very well have a set of convictions that says it is wrong to take drugs, but if he simply makes the decision as an adolescent seventeen-year-old boy, he is more likely to think, "Why not? I'll go for it!" But if he makes the decision based on who he will become, he has a lot better chance of making a good decision. He may even ask himself, "Could this get in the way of my purpose in life?" If the answer to that question is yes, he'll decide accordingly.

The bottom line is this: a strong sense of life purpose will always lead to better decisions. And as parents, we are the purveyors of purpose. We've been given the golden opportunity to instill into our kids purpose and destiny.

THE STEPS TO PURPOSE

If we, as parents, are convinced that we must build purpose into our kids' lives, there are a few steps to follow to ensure that purpose is highlighted and affirmed. These are

- Know your own purpose
- Write a Family Mission Statement
- Know the power of your words
- Enjoy the purpose of the present

Know Your Own Purpose

Have you ever asked your teen, "Why did you do that?" only to be answered with a shrug? Or grilled them with a "What were you thinking?" and received "I don't know, I just did it" in response? When we get answers like that from our teenagers, we throw up our hands in frustration and retreat into some rationalization about the nature of all teenagers.

But if we'll think about it, we'll find that we are often the same way. Many of us have never firmly established in our minds, or in the minds of our family members, why we are doing what we are doing. Why do I need a promotion that will take more time away from home but give us more money? What will that achieve in my life's plan? Why do I need another new car? What is the purpose of my life? Why did I have to buy that dress that was on sale? Why am I alive? Why am I working? Why do I care?

Now, think with us for a minute. Too many of us are living for money, reputation, property, the kids, our marriages, a better education, travel, or whatever, only to discover that the problems at home still await. We haven't asked ourselves basic questions that might realign our priorities. Why do I want more money? What would I do with it if I had more? Why do I need a good reputation with my peers or in my community? What do I want to do with the influence that a good reputation will bring me? Why do I need a new car and a nicer house? Image? Is personal comfort my purpose in life? Do I live for physical pleasure, or is there a reason why I need a place to relax? Why do I want my kids to be great? Why am I married? Am I married because I want to be married or because I want to care for my spouse? Am I married for intimacy or for companionship?

None of the things that are mentioned in these questions are necessarily good or bad. You may very well need a new car for your family's safety and transportation ease. You may need a good reputation so that you can have opportunities to serve your community. You may need a place to relax so that you can be rejuvenated to be a better employee, spouse, or parent. The point is to ask the questions that define your purpose. If you are spending time doing things that don't meet your purpose in life, then why are you doing them?

As you read this section, keep in mind that building purpose doesn't happen overnight. Don't expect to put this book down, fall asleep, and wake up in the morning with clear vision. People redefine and reexamine their purpose all the time, and it takes a great while to really understand your purpose. Every one of us needs to develop the habit of regularly pausing and thinking about our purpose. Why did God create mankind? What is his plan for our lives? What is his plan for my life? Does he have one? Am I fulfilling it? The point is that if we can answer those questions, we will know exactly how to live.

Write a Family Mission Statement

A family is more than a mom and a dad with children. A family is a unit that should be doing something and going somewhere for a reason. People have purpose, and so do families. When we don't know what our purpose is, our families are aimless, our children are aimless, and there is no deep compelling reason for us to stay together. Before proposing to Gayle, Ted thought carefully about the purpose of having a family.

When I proposed to Gayle, I knew that I wanted to live with her the rest of my life, but I also knew that if we didn't have purpose together, the marriage would not be complete. I didn't think I was a great enough man to keep Gayle happy all of her life, but I knew that a great purpose could pull the two of us together for a lifetime. So when I proposed, I told her everything I knew about God's plan for my life and then asked her, "Would you like to be part of this plan?" When she said that she would, I said, "Then would you marry me?"

Three months later we were married. As the years passed, we wrote a mission statement for our lives. Our

union, the two of us together, now has a well-defined purpose that gives us a reason for going to work, enjoying our
evenings, resting and growing. We had to have direction and
reason. Our mission statement, which took months to write
and is revisited every few years, had to be written.

When we started having children, we knew they were
born into more than a family, they were born into a purpose.
We are convinced that children are a gift that enhances a family's purpose. On Mondays we have Family Night, and at
times we'll talk about our purpose as a family, which explains
why we do what we do and defines who we are as a group.
All of the family members are individuals who have distinct
gifts, experiences, and roles, but we are all one. We have the
same last name for a reason. We live in the same house for a
reason. Each person's individual purpose works in harmony
with our family's purpose. This gives value and direction to
the family.

When our kids hear us discussing purpose, they are inspired to
think of purpose in their own lives. When the family mission statement has settled deep within them, they will use it as a plumb line
for decisions in their lives. The friends they choose, the hobbies
they embrace, their performance in school, and the decisions they
make away from home can all be gently but resolutely guided by
our family mission statement.

Stephen R. Covey, in his book *The 7 Habits of Highly Effective
Families*, contends that all families should function according to their
mission statement. A family mission statement, writes Covey, "is a
combined, unified expression from all family members of what
your family is all about—what it is you really want to do and be—
and the principles you choose to govern your family life."[2] A family mission statement answers the question "Why are we a family?"
Once that answer is established, the family's purpose answers all
the other questions about what the members of the family do or do
not do. Do we smoke? Do we steal? Do we lie to each other? Does

Dad or Mom take regular, extensive trips away from the family? What church do we attend? What do we do on the weekends? How do we save money, and for what reason?

Not long ago, Ted and Gayle decided it was time to revisit their family mission statement. They met with their kids and told each of them to take some time and think about their personal purposes in life. Why did they think they were created? What were their dreams, and how were they going to achieve those dreams? Then, on a given night, the Haggards met together at the dining room table and read to each other their personal mission statements. As each person read their purpose, the family members discussed that purpose, talking about how they could encourage each other toward those goals and how they could incorporate it into the overall family mission statement. At the end of the evening, Christy and Marcus, the two oldest children, gathered together all the notes and personal mission statements in order to combine them into an entire family mission statement.

Actually, both of us have done the same thing. John and his wife, Sarah, have one young son, but they know their family mission statement, and they are planning on answering his questions in life according to that mission statement. When questions arise, they need only to refer to their mission statement to point them toward the answer.

A family mission statement, which can hang on the wall or refrigerator, might look something like this:

Our family mission is to:
Love each other deeply and sincerely;
Support each other in the pursuit of our goals;
Pray for each other daily;
Always use words of encouragement instead of abuse;
Make guests feel welcome into our home;
Meet the needs of those around us, whether in the home, church, community, or world;
Create a heritage of hope, love, and perseverance.

As Covey says, the family mission statement provides us with "a destination and a compass." We know where we are going, and we know the direction we need to take to get there.

For teenagers, the benefits here are limitless. A mission statement provides the elements of direction—if direction is absent from a teen's life, they fall easily into poor choices. The family mission statement helps them to answer the question of purpose, because the first step in writing a family mission statement is to have each member decide what their personal mission should be. It helps them to make moral decisions, because they know they are living for something greater than the moment. It helps them make wise choices about the future, and perhaps most importantly, it helps them understand that home is always a place they can call "home."

Know the Power of Your Words

"'Worthless! You're worthless!' That's all I remember my dad saying. His voice is still crystal clear to me. Those were the words that my dad would say to me over and over. Look, I couldn't take it anymore. I don't care. I just don't care. Forget it."

We sat in the booth at Village Inn with nothing to say. This time, we knew, it would be best to just listen. Mike, a local seventeen-year-old, had called Ted at 2:00 A.M. and asked to meet him here. After a cup of coffee and half a bottle of Visine, we caught up with Mike in the corner of the smoking section.

Mike said there was a warrant out for his arrest. Before we convinced Mike to turn himself in, we listened to his story. Mike grew up in a family full of violence and hatred. He recalled for us in vivid word pictures the verbal and physical abuse he suffered at the hands of his father. As we watched him suck at his cigarette with a hard look in his eyes, we knew Mike's tragic childhood had made him the way he was. It didn't seem fair. Mike should be happy, outgoing, and dreaming of college, but instead he was another hurting teenager, bitter at life and about to be sent to prison. The years that should be full of new jobs, new dreams, and new girlfriends were being ripped from him before he had a chance—mostly because he had heard his father tell him all his life that he was a failure, doomed to a life of despair.

We know that it's easy to point to a tough childhood as an excuse for bad decisions later in life. Without question, personal responsibility trumps our situation in life, regardless of how tough it might be. But it is undeniable that the words that are spoken to us growing up deeply affect the way we live our lives. In layman's terms, what goes in, eventually comes out. Our actions and reactions are largely determined by the things we have seen and heard throughout our lives. It's pretty simple, really. If we are subjected to violence and hateful words, those things are planted in us, much like a seed, and will eventually come back out of us in one form or another.

Mike's story, unfortunately, is a dime a dozen. But it is typical of so many teens who fail to find purpose in their lives. If your children hear you telling them that they are destined to succeed, that you believe in them, that you love them unconditionally, they are likely to have a huge amount of confidence built inside of them. If, on the other hand, they rarely hear you encourage them, or even worse, they hear you discourage them or make fun of their efforts, you can count on their failure (or at least their resentment).

Speak life, vision, and hope to your kids. Tell them you believe in them. As much as possible, let them know you love them. If they hear your words of life, they will automatically gravitate toward a positive and specific purpose for their lives.

Enjoy the Purpose of the Present

While we have been so passionately writing about purpose, we've been looking forward to one fantastic little counterpoint to put this great principle in perspective. Even when we are thinking of overall mission statements, goals for the future, and distant dreams, we must bear in mind that the present moment, right now, is our greatest opportunity for parenting. Sometimes, we run the risk of thinking so much of who our children are going to "turn out to be," that we neglect to enjoy our fourteen-year-old playing basketball in the driveway or our sixteen-year-old getting ready for homecoming.

Grandparents often tell young moms to enjoy their children in their various stages, only to have the exhausted mother sigh as she thinks of late nights, early mornings, and long days of breaking toys, running late, and whining. But grandparents have learned something: they have learned that life is not about waiting to get to the next stage, the next house, or the next promotion. People who have lived well know that purpose not only directs your future, but also gives value to the present. Purpose lets you stop and breathe, love and embrace, and look lovingly into a child's eyes. Ever take a drive through an old part of town and notice all the elderly men sitting out on the front porch, smoking pipes, slowly talking, and drinking Mason jars of lemonade? These men are not just retired, they are men who have learned how to enjoy life.

We are so busy during our twenties preparing to be thirty that we don't value our twenties until they are gone. Then, when we are in our thirties we feel a little old, and we're starting to get a little fat, so we wish we were in our twenties again, but we're too busy to do much about it because we're preparing for our forties. When our forties come, we've got to make a lot of money to pay for college expenses for our kids and retirement expenses for us, and now we have reading glasses and our knees ache a little, so we long for our thirties, but have to eat right to prepare for our fifties. On and on the cycle goes. Soon, we find ourselves old, tired, and lonely, wondering where life went and expecting to find a list of accomplishments or travels to justify our lives.

But that rationale misses the point. Life isn't just going somewhere and doing something. Life is relationships. It is enjoying the day, working and laughing with a friend. Shut off the television and stop wasting life by watching others live—get out and live life yourself. Breathe, smell, gaze at the sky, listen to the birds. As a parent, this means embracing your children while they are young. Enjoying the spilled milk, the late night fevers, the children sleeping in your bed because they are scared.

We suggest keeping a list of the most meaningful moments in life. Ted's list includes moments like eating a simple lunch with his oldest son, Marcus, on a small sand island off the coast of Zanzibar between scuba dives into the coral reef, crying with his daughter over her dying horse, quietly holding Gayle's hand while driving, and walking with a friend on the beach in New Zealand. Life is special for Ted because Alex likes traveling, Elliott likes laughing, and Jonathan likes cuddling. It would be terrible to just pass through these moments. It's part of who we are to stop, take a deep breath, and live.

Purpose cannot be discovered or defined for our futures until we can do it now. Right now. In this moment, this hour, this day. By being content with the great things and the little things. Once we're content, then we can project into the future and decide why we are here and where we are going. But if we don't stop and live, life will be stolen from us by urgent matters.

What does this have to do with being a confident parent? Everything. It is worth our time to learn the secrets of enjoying parenthood. Not only will we be happier but we will create a mood in our home of freshness, security, and trust. Our kids will love seeing us laugh easily, they will enjoy sharing their lives with us, and they will be free to discover the wonderful purpose for their lives.

CHAPTER
Four

Guard Their Minds:
Aim the Lamp

Merely having an open mind is nothing. The object of opening the mind, as of opening the mouth, is to shut it again on something solid.

G. K. CHESTERTON

The young man shuffled into our offices looking as if he had lost his way home. His head was tucked deeply between his shoulders. Meeting us for the first time, he wouldn't dare look us in the eyes. Softly, carefully, he introduced himself as David and stated, very plainly, that he was at the end of his rope. He needed help. Something was wrong. Something deep. Something secret. Until now.

In the safety of our offices, David told us about his struggle with sexual addiction. Where many young men brag about and exaggerate their virile encounters with the opposite sex, David wasn't at all proud of what he had done. Clenching the sides of his chair, he told the details of his living nightmare. Only a year before, he had logged onto the Internet one night to read movie reviews and check the scores of college basketball games. On one of the Web sites, he noticed an enticing link to another site, offering pictures of swimsuit models. "Innocent enough," he told himself, not knowing that this simple step would lead to the greatest struggle of his life.

Like most young men, David felt as though he shouldn't dig deeper, but the pull was stronger than his resolve. Soft porn led to hard-core porn, hard-core porn led to an addiction that dominated his life. Night after night, he logged onto his computer and hosted thousands of pornographic images, unable to stop himself. He was laden with guilt and sometimes would stay off the computer for a day or so. But he'd always go back. He couldn't quit, or wouldn't quit. Regardless, he didn't quit, and now this drive was controlling his life.

After a while, the images weren't enough. David began clicking into live chat rooms to talk about sex with other people. Then, one cold December night, he took a step into the world he had promised himself he would never enter. During a chat room session that night, he was invited to meet a girl, live and in person. He told himself it was a bad idea and tried not to think about it. An hour passed. Then he told himself it was a good idea. The battle raged in his mind for days, until he found himself standing at her door. . . .

Over the next several months, David's world changed. He began to experiment with sex with a variety of people he met online. After every encounter he wanted to stop, but he also wanted more. Finally, he found his way into our office. "I wish I had never logged on," he sobbed, tears rolling down his cheeks. "I wish computers had never been invented." For three hours, we talked with him, prayed with him, and constructed a plan to help him.

That day, the power of images was clear. That day, there was no debate over the impact of certain forms of entertainment. David, and thousands like him, can tell you, without a doubt, that the things we see affect the things we do.

WHO RAISES OUR KIDS — US OR THE MEDIA?

Within hours of the Littleton tragedy, parents, lawmakers, and newspaper columnists were blaming the entertainment media for the massacre. All the usual suspects were lined up, from Marilyn

Manson to *Natural Born Killers* to violent video games such as *Doom*. Of course, the reason for the tragedy in Colorado lies much deeper and is much more complex than video games and R-rated movies, but the heart-wrenching event reminded us all of the ancient proverb: "Our eyes are the window to our souls."

Philosophers, educators, psychologists, and theologians are constantly revising their opinions of the impact of what we see and hear. Much of formal education is based on the influence of books and videos. We have invested billions of dollars to create interesting ways of providing information to young people. Though the debate continues on how much these things affect us, we all know the truth: input, whether from books, music videos, the Internet, or a friend, is what forms us. We are influenced by the ideas we've assimilated.

Given the current technological and entertainment onslaught, the fact that input shapes us means two different things: first, it means that we are living in the greatest age in the history of the world because so much information is available; and second, it means we are living in the most dangerous age in the history of the world. Consider this: in a single day, a young person can sit in Barnes and Noble reading *The Grapes of Wrath* for a couple of hours, then head over to the Cineplex and watch the latest Quentin Tarantino flick, where the women are sex objects and the men are greedy, murderous fools (but the movie is a *comedy*), then go home, turn up the digital stereo and log onto the Internet, where they can either finish research for their John Steinbeck essay or, just as easily, download pornographic pictures or learn how to make a bomb.

What are we, as parents, to do? We want our teens to be able to use all the educational and entertainment tools available to them, but how do we monitor their choices? How can we ensure that our kids read the right books, see the right movies, listen to the right music, and use the Internet wisely?

Do we ostracize them from all entertainment? No. Do we trust them to make good choices away from home? Sometimes.

These are perplexing questions, and there is a host of experts available to answer them. After situations like Littleton, print media is filled with the typical articles and statistics on how to control your kids, how to restrict their access to sensory input, how to get them into counseling when they go astray. This information is helpful, but we have to remember that kids, fundamentally, are raised by their *parents*. That may sound trite, but in this generation, it is profound. We are the ones who must be there for them. Know them. Love them. Guide them. Parenting is a full-time job, and it requires constant effort. This conclusion is true whether you are reacting to a tragedy like Littleton or living out a normal week, and it is certainly true when dealing with entertainment choices.

In a recent article in *Time,* Daniel Okrent offered this telling analysis:

> Consider this picture: a kid sits alone in front of his computer, cruising the Internet. In the background a CD player blares misogynistic obscenities. In another room, the television features a teenage heroine contemplating violence against her classmates. The local sixplex is playing a film that spills more blood than a slaughterhouse hoses down in a month. And, in most states, if you can't buy a gun with a few phone calls and a couple of hundred bucks, you haven't really tried.
>
> Now you go into that kid's room, unplug the computer and walk out. What have you really accomplished?[3]

The idea that parenting requires more than rules and regulations, even when it comes to guarding entertainment choices, is so simple that it is obvious, but so many of us fail in this area that constant reminders are necessary (we, the authors, remind each other every week). Ted says it took a revelation for him to learn this lesson, and it changed his whole perspective on parenting:

> I remember when it happened to me. I was sitting in a first-class seat of a United Airlines jumbo jet flying to one more dream engagement. Everything was working for me. I was making more money than my dad ever dreamed of, was well accepted by my peers, and I had some Christian lead-

ers projecting that the next twenty-five years would go very well for me. But while thinking about the talk I was going to give that evening, it dawned on me. "What am I doing? My kids will never be this age again. I'll never be able to get this day back again, and I'm spending it with strangers instead of my family. The people I'm going to speak to will not come to my funeral, visit me in the hospital when I get sick, or support my kids financially if things ever go wrong."

As I was thinking this, I turned to the businessman sitting next to me and told him that I was finished, done, through. As soon as I completed my current schedule of engagements, I was staying home. And, if work required me to travel like this, I would quit. He looked at me with astonishment as I emphasized, "I would rather live in a mud hut with my kids than have them in a nice home without me. I don't want to meet my kids when they are old. I don't want to invite them to a baseball game when they are the ones who are too busy. I want to camp out with them, eat dinner with them, go to church with them, lay in the yard and look at the clouds with them. But they're at home right now and I'm not. I'm finished. I quit."

As I talked, the man behind us leaned forward and said that he was quitting too. He explained that he had a heart attack the year before, but the company talked him into working a few more years before retirement. He knew he was dying—alone. He'd already missed the chance to know his kids. He wondered if they really loved him, or if they only loved the things he'd provided. He grinned at us as he said, "I'm going to finish this trip and find a way to stay home. I'll still travel some, but not like this. I'm going home."

You would think we were having a religious revival in the front of the airplane. That day, all of us had come to understand the value of a Dad.

When we decide to raise our own kids, we find that areas like entertainment are less threatening. If we are truly involved in our teens' lives, monitoring sensory input is a natural part of the parent-teen relationship. Since it is always important to have practical guidelines for the family to follow, however, let's discuss a few parameters that we have set up for our own families.

ENTERTAINMENT GUIDELINES THAT WORK

1. Outside Is Better Than Inside

There is an old Midwestern proverb about daughters: "Your daughter will either fall in love with a boy or with a horse. I suggest you buy a horse." With this in mind, Ted bought his daughter, Christy, a horse, and she has spent much of her adolescence outside working with her horses and other animals. Instead of coming home from school and flipping channels and talking on the phone in her room, Christy usually goes outside after school to care for her animals.

We encourage families to intentionally develop an outdoor life. We like to use the saying: "It takes forty acres to raise a child." Helping teens appreciate the outdoors is as simple as doing outdoor activities with them. If they enjoy hiking with Dad, playing Frisbee at family picnics, and playing catch in the front yard, they will be inclined to develop outdoor hobbies. Go carts, riding lawn mowers, animals, neighborhood basketball, horseback riding, and working as a family in the yard all make outside living more fun. Our families like to lay on the grass and look at the sky, create shapes out of the clouds, listen to the sounds of the season, and feel the fresh air. We have great memories of camping with our families, and we also have our share of camping trips from hell. Both are equally memorable. Our basic rule is that outside events are better than inside events—if your teens are outside playing soccer, you can be sure that they aren't watching seedy movies on television.

2. Value Sports

As children grow, they will likely go through at least one season when they want to be involved with team sports. With the right coach and the right approach, sports can be one of the most significant influences in teaching a young person how to be successful. Team sports are a microcosm of adult life. They teach healthy competition, teamwork, excellence, the satisfaction of a job well done, and the character to recover from defeat.

Through sports our teens learn to bond with others, to enjoy the adventure of a near-win, and to shape the discipline of wanting to win at all costs while having to follow rules. We love to encourage our kids to play sports when they become interested in them—snowboarding, baseball, basketball, mountain biking, soccer, paint ball, football—the list is long and exciting. After every game of mud volleyball, when the entire family is covered in mud, laughing and joking with each other, it's good for all of us. Sports often leave positive and powerful memories. They bond people together.

As important as the sport itself is the management of emotions that has to be learned to enjoy sports. In team sports, our kids can go from being reserved, detached, and hardened to being expressive, affectionate, and resilient. Sports open them and help them discover their authenticity. Simply put, sports help kids learn to be happy.

3. Value Music

A kid's first piano lessons are either their first steps toward a love affair with music or a horrible childhood memory. The teacher, the atmosphere, and our response to their music either give our kids the encouragement to develop an appreciation for music or shame them into hating it. We must be careful to respond the right way—if we do it right, we can give them a gift that will last a lifetime.

The vast majority of teens listen to music constantly. Through music, they can learn to bond with others, form an identity, and express themselves. Ted's oldest son, Marcus, loves music. He plays the piano, saxophone, guitar, and clarinet. He loves jazz, gospel, movie sound tracks, and Glen Miller—style big-band swing. He has won several awards for swing dancing, and his room keeps the whole house full of music. Marcus's love for music has given him a group, a reputation, a role. When the youth group at church went to Nepal, he was part of the band. He added value to the team—music connected him.

To ensure that your teens make good choices about which bands to listen to, get them into an environment where they can learn the importance of positive listening habits and then model appropriate listening habits yourself. Don't alienate them with music that is too outdated or irrelevant, and enjoy introducing them to your favorite music. Just make music an overall positive experience for your teen. Focus on the Family, in Colorado Springs, offers age-appropriate magazines, books, tapes, and videos to help teens make wise decisions about music. We highly recommend these materials for all families.

4. Build Big Ideas

All civilizations have a series of big ideas or themes that form their foundation for life. Western Civilization is the product of thought about a variety of subjects. As children grow into teenagers and enter into their college years, they often enjoy talking about major philosophies and ideologies that form our world. We must embrace this opportunity to discuss these ideas, because doing so will give our teenagers a context and reason for life. In our families, we talk about these ideas after watching a movie or while sitting around a campfire. While traveling through different countries, we'll discuss wealth and poverty, royal families and elected governments, and free markets and command economies. The trick is to have an intuitive sense of what your kids are interested in, and then find ways to transition into conversations about big ideas. Below is a list of twenty-five one-word big ideas that represent entire systems of thought:

Art
Courage
Democracy
Desire
Emotion

Eternity
Family
Freedom
God
Good and Evil
Government
History
Honor
Justice
Mathematics
Mechanics
Pleasure and Pain
Logic
Science
Sin
Time
Truth
Virtue
War and Peace
Wisdom

5. Place the Computer in a High-Traffic Area

We put our family computers in a high-traffic place, such as a wide hallway, not in a private room. This is important. Ted has a seventeen-year-old daughter and four sons, ages sixteen, eleven, eight, and six, who all like the Internet and have specialized educational programs that they use on the computer. With the adult controls activated and the computer out in the open, we can remain relatively sure of the input that comes into our families.

6. Equip Your Television with a Programming Control System

Direct TV gives parents the ability to place a rating limit on all programming. You can purchase Direct TV or an equivalent system and set it so that the only shows that can be viewed are rated G, PG, and PG13. You can have hundreds of channels and still be confident that no R-rated, NC–17, or X programs come into the home. For normal television viewing, V-chip technology is readily available, or you can just check the television listings, which now show the ratings for all shows.

7. Make Your Home a Fun Place to Be

Do all you can to make your home the kind of place where other kids would want to come, so that your teenager's friends are coming to your house, instead of your teenager always staying at other people's homes. That way, you are always aware of their environment.

8. Pay Attention to Your Teen's Video-Game Habits

Over the past twenty-five years, video games and video-game machines have become a staple in almost every teenager's room. Without question, the challenge and thrill of on-screen competition is alluring. Video games can be entertaining, educational, and skill-enhancing. But they can also be unnecessarily violent, overtly sexual, and addictive. Many teens play video games at the expense of studies, social activities, and sleep. If your teen is a big video-game fan, help him or her select games that will challenge them to think, and monitor the amount of time they spend playing them. Help them avoid games that will enforce negative attitudes or actions. Like movies and CDs, many video games are also rated. Look for these ratings to help you make good decisions in selecting appropriate and fun games for your teen.

Remember, when it comes to setting parameters for your teens, it's important to keep open lines of communication throughout the process. As you make decisions that limit entertainment options for your teen, talk to your kids about why. It's easy to simply say no and leave your reasons ambiguous. Don't be afraid to dialogue about the effects of input and the reasons to avoid certain material and encourage other media.

Modeling is important in this process. Your entertainment habits will influence your children's entertainment habits. If you read, their chances of enjoying reading are increased. If you watch movies they are not permitted to watch, you will create a conflict. Our standard is that if there is anyone in the house that something is unacceptable for, everyone in the house should avoid it. This standard communicates integrity and keeps the adults from embittering the younger family members. It builds consistency and mutual respect. It helps create a healthy atmosphere throughout the home—a pleasant fragrance.

THE FLIP SIDE

A few weeks ago, Jay Leno attempted a short experiment to get a few laughs. He gathered together famous quotes from history and well-known TV commercial songs and slogans. He grabbed a camera and took to the streets. The results of his on-street survey were both hilarious and horrifying.

He walked up to a young girl and asked her to finish the historical quote: "I regret that I have but ..." The girl had no idea how to finish, so she made up an answer like, "A few dollars to spend on new clothes." Of course, she'd gotten it wrong. Then Jay said, "It's 'The quicker picker upper.'" Without hesitating, the girl said confidently, "Bounty paper towels." Jay's next victim was a man in his early twenties. Again, he asked the young man to finish the quotation: "Don't fire until you see the ..." The young man thought for a minute and then said, "The big tanks coming"? Once again, wrong. Then he was asked, "Who is 'The Freshmaker'?" The young man quickly replied, "Mentos."

Six or seven more people were approached, each with similar results. Jay's laughs were earned, and a harrowing point was made. We read too few books, and watch too much television.

The flip side to all the parenting advice on monitoring teens' input is something we don't often hear today: the best way to guard your teenager's mind is to encourage him or her to read as much as possible. Buy them books. Take them to the library. Go onto an online bookstore with them and search for their favorite titles. Read together and discuss. In short, do everything you can to encourage your teens' intellectual pursuits. Doing so will help them learn to think critically about all their sensory input, and reading the right books will shape their minds at a fantastic rate.

We can't emphasize enough the importance of good literature in the hands of your teenagers. Many of the greatest leaders in history earned their education not through a systematic educational system, but through books. Abraham Lincoln was a self-taught man who gained the majority of his knowledge through reading. Books and the ideas that are communicated in them are not only valuable but necessary. As we are pulled quickly toward the third millennium, be sure that your teens have a strong grasp of the people, events, and ideas that have guided us on our voyage of history. If young people will be committed to reading good books, they will not only educate themselves beyond their peers, but they will place themselves in a position to become future leaders in their spheres of influence.

Of course, books are only one way to help your teens shape their minds. In addition to reading, help them discover the wonders of all art forms: the theater, visual art, artistic films, and fine music offer whole worlds waiting to be explored by young (and old) minds. Spending a day together at an art museum or attending an evening play will create experiences your teen won't soon forget, and it will whet their appetites for invaluable intellectual pursuits.

All of our children have light in their lives, so as we walk with our teenagers through their formative years, it's our privilege to help them "aim the lamp" of their minds toward the things that really matter. Light without focus can dim, lose purpose, and ultimately go out. But as parents, we can brighten and aim their lamps by protecting them from potentially negative input and by encouraging them to read, watch, and assimilate ideas that have already proven their positive impact on our world.

CHAPTER
Five

Shape Their Character: The Ten Commandments for Parents of Teens

If you think about what you ought to do for other people, your character will take care of itself.

WOODROW WILSON

Michelangelo is regarded as one of the greatest sculptors in history. On his famous sculptures, he spent countless days, weeks, and months meticulously analyzing every crucial detail. Today, in museums throughout Europe, his work is on display for tourists to admire, art critics to curiously inspect, and other artists to envy. But right next to his beautiful completed sculptures lie forty ironic footnotes to his triumphant career. Of the fifty sculptures Michelangelo initiated in his lifetime, only ten were finished. Forty pieces of work were left undone. Forty reminders of unrealized potential. Forty hints that the greatness we see was only a portion of his genius.

Of course, only a fool would criticize Michelangelo for laziness. But looking at his unfinished pieces evokes an eerie longing as one can imagine what the completed works might have looked like.

Michelangelo may have taken his best ideas to the grave with him, leaving us with a few dozen blocks of marble with a leg sticking out here, a shoulder there.

As we raise our kids, we are more than just passive observers, praying and hoping that our teens turn out okay. We are artists. Our teenagers are the statues, and we are the sculptors with hammers and chisels. In our hands lies the opportunity to finish the job, to create human beings who realize the full extent of their potential. Parenting is a time of intense concentration and anguished study of every detail of our kids' lives. As they grow through success and failure we must be ready to apply a little brushup, perhaps some polish, and maybe knock a chip away every now and then.

Shaping a teenager's character is a time of trial and error. It takes grit, determination, and focus. It takes resilience. It takes parents. But take heart: while the journey is long, the payoff is without parallel. In building their character, we are directing them toward a life of success. Shaping character is the single greatest way to help our teenagers avoid making heartbreaking decisions under the fire of peer pressure and confusing social signals. Shaping their character equips them with the integrity to make the right choices and the confidence to know how to live well. Aristotle said, "To enjoy the things we ought, and to hate the things we ought, has the greatest bearing on excellence of character." It's our responsibility to raise our kids to know right from wrong, and to know *why* right is right and wrong is wrong. Those lessons are learned in the fire of character formation. If we can learn to build their character, we can rest at ease while they are out making decisions on their own. With a solid character base, the questions teenagers face in a typical week ("Should I go out with this guy alone?" "Would it be okay to go to that party this weekend?") are not as threatening as they once seemed.

"Okay, so how do we do it?" Funny you should ask . . .

DIGGING OUT THE TEN COMMANDMENTS (THEY STILL APPLY)

One of the reasons the Bible continues to be so popular is because it applies to every segment of our lives. Have a question about finances? Love? Your boss? The Bible deals with it all, and it is especially helpful in the area of parenting. In fact, the Ten Commandments alone (Exodus 20:2–17) provide a wealth of information for raising kids. Below, we have listed a version of the Ten Commandments for the parents of teenagers. When it comes to building character, this is the best information available.

Commandment 1: Live with eternity in mind.
("Thou shalt have no other gods before Me.")
Commandment 2: Life is more than friends, money, and material things.
("Thou shalt have no graven images.")
Commandment 3: Use your words well.
("Thou shalt not take the Lord's name in vain.")
Commandment 4: Use your time well.
("Thou shalt remember the Sabbath day, and keep it holy.")
Commandment 5: Respect your mom and your dad.
("Honor thy mother and thy father.")
Commandment 6: Value people.
("Thou shalt not murder.")
Commandment 7: Discipline your sexuality.
("Thou shalt not commit adultery.")
Commandment 8: Earn your own way.
("Thou shalt not steal.")
Commandment 9: Tell the truth.
("Thou shalt not bear false witness.")
Commandment 10: Be grateful for what you have.
("Thou shalt not covet.")

Commandment 1: Live with eternity in mind.
("Thou shalt have no other gods before Me.")

In a world bent on me-ism—the theory that we should have whatever we want, whenever we want—God and eternity have little or no place. As parents, we can change that. As we train our kids to honor God, even if we don't understand everything about God ourselves, we set them up for success.

One of the reasons respect for God makes us better people is because it keeps us from being shortsighted. God forces us to think about eternity because he has given us a proposition for eternal life. When we live with eternal life in mind, we realize that our time on earth must be invested, not spent. We begin to care for the poor, protect orphans and widows, and serve the less fortunate. Taking a pie to a sick neighbor and mowing the lawn of an elderly friend are responses to a fundamental belief that compassion matters, because eternity is a fact.

But our society sends several messages that have given our kids permission to be shortsighted, to place other gods before God and his eternal perspective. One such message is "Man is the measure of all things." This was the mantra of the Renaissance era, and it has produced a blight in our era. We've all seen it and heard it, on bumper stickers, television ads, and, no doubt, from our teens. "What is right for you isn't necessarily right for me." "Be your own god." This philosophy has proven to be devastating over and over again. When we believe that we are our own gods, we can determine right and wrong for ourselves with no thought to God or anyone else. That is why people often end up hurting other people if they accept this philosophy. When we, as humans, determine who will live and who will die, who will prosper and who will suffer, without any external eternal standard, we make too many mistakes. Mankind hasn't proven a worthy god. We are often selfish and wicked, all too willing to hurt the other person for our own good. We are not good gods. But God is a good God, which is why he wants us to remember him.

You can make a laundry list of other gods: sex, money, a career, popularity. You need not look far to find people who have given their lives for these things. There's no doubt that they are tempting; indeed, they are essentially good. But if we live for them, and if we teach our kids to live for them, we can be sure that we are starting our children on an empty path. Those things are all temporary, not eternal.

One last god worth mentioning is the god of happiness. If our children believe that right and wrong are subservient to their personal happiness, then sacrificing for another's good, giving to the poor, defending justice for the benefit of someone else, or simply mowing the grass for a sick neighbor is unimportant. But happiness, like money and popularity, is temporary. Jesus told us that to find life we have to lose it, which was his paradoxical way of saying that the focus of our lives must not exclusively be our own emotional and physical well-being but the emotional and physical well-being of others as well. When we consider eternity and give our lives away, we find true life.

Commandment 2: Life is more than friends, money, and material things. ("Thou shalt have no graven images.")

Everyone worships something. We build buildings and admire and serve them. We serve our favorite sports team with our time, money, and clothes. If we let our passion for "stuff" outweigh our passion for God and our families, we will end up living for "stuff." God doesn't want us to worship or serve his creation—he wants us to know the joy of worshiping the Creator himself. He wants to give us things, but he doesn't want things to control our affections. We've all seen people completely lose their tempers over a ding on their car in a parking lot, a dropped pass at a football game, or the discovery of a questionable business deal. When we teach our kids that life is summed up in those things instead of teaching them that life is about God, family, close friends, and helping people, we may be teaching them to be tyrants.

Many of us remember when President Johnson was launching his national initiative to eliminate poverty in America. One of his reasons for the War on Poverty was the belief that if we could eliminate poverty, we could also eliminate crime in America. Not true. Prosperity is better than poverty, to be sure, but prosperity doesn't make people good. Virtually every school shooting has been committed in an affluent area. We don't become good when we prosper—we become good when we use our prosperity to serve others.

When we give it away. When we refuse to worship things. When we live for the good of others rather than focusing everything on ourselves. This makes us good, and it makes our kids great.

Commandment 3: Use your words well.
("Thou shalt not take the Lord's name in vain.")

Ted's seven-year-old son, Elliot, has never heard a person use profanity except on television. A few weeks ago, Elliot saw one of his little friends in the hallway of the church; walking toward him, Elliot put his hands in his pockets John Wayne–style and casually called out, "What the hell are you doing here?" The other little boy's mom was around the corner, and she laughed with relief that cute little Elliot had some spunk.

Elliot doesn't cuss anymore. We don't need to explain here how he received his revelation on using words well, but now his favorite word is "loquacious."

It has been said that "words are the fabric of life." They can create, heal, or destroy. Words are some of the most powerful weapons we possess, and we must teach our teenagers the value of the spoken word. Learning what is right and appropriate in speech is just as important as learning what is right and appropriate in actions. After Eric Harris and Dylan Klebold went through their school happily shooting other students, we were all shocked to learn that much of their motivation to kill was the hatred that stirred in them because other students had verbally mocked them. Unfortunately, they didn't just respond with words but with action.

Fight the temptation to use profanity around your teenager. Profanity not only demonstrates for them that such language is acceptable, but it reveals your own lack of discipline and skill at handling the English language. Be sure to do what you say you are going to do. If you say you will be at the soccer game, be there. If you tell your teenage girl that she is grounded for two weeks, keep her grounded for two weeks.

Language is a great gift. As parents and leaders of young people, we can model appropriate language, or we can teach them how to use words to hurt people and devalue things. For example, when we take the Lord's name in vain, we are carelessly using words to devalue someone who is holy. When our kids hear this, they will use words poorly as well. We must teach teens to be careful with their words. Some words are holy, others are common. Some words communicate general concepts, others are precise. Some words encourage people to achieve, other discourage people. Some words teach people to love one another, others denote the mechanics and tone of hate. If we teach our children to speak well, they can learn how to live well.

Commandment 4: Use your time well.
("Thou shalt remember the Sabbath day, and keep it holy.")

Many of us are so busy charging ahead in life, working overtime to provide a great life for our families and joining every club and committee, that we miss the value of rest and reflection. Taking time to pause and reflect on life is a lesson that needs to be taught and modeled. Whether that time is spent at church or quietly with family and friends, slowing down to adjust priorities is extremely valuable. Time is our most precious commodity. Even God took a day to look at what he had created, enjoy it, and reflect on what was to come.

Several years ago, we performed two funerals in a week's time. Both were for fifty-eight-year-old men, but the men had lived very different lives. The first funeral had to be held in a stadium to accommodate the thousands of people who came to pay their respects. This man had given his life for others, was admired by the masses, and when cancer took his life, the masses remembered and honored him. The second funeral was attended by four people. Before the funeral, we received a call from the police department warning us to be careful about what we said during the funeral because the people attending were probably armed and were certainly angry. The four people there hated each other, and they hated the person they were burying. Their faces were hard and full of resentment as they waited for the service to finish so they could argue over the man's possessions.

Both of those men had fifty-eight years to live. The former man invested his time well; the latter spent his time foolishly. The former man valued people, and thoughtfully utilized his time. The latter man never rested, never made time to play with his kids and sit around and talk casually with his wife.

Popular wisdom always encourages us to spend quality time with our kids. We obviously believe that is great advice, but in our experience, the only way to find quality time is to invest a large quantity of it. With great investments come great rewards. Time with our families is invaluable—it's the only way we can model life. As we invest time and model the wise use of time, our kids will have parameters for their use of time. If your kids see you watching television, drinking with your friends, and sleeping late in the mornings, they will learn those patterns for spending time. If, on the other hand, they see you reading great books and talking about them, exercising and relaxing with your spouse and children, and enjoying friends of the family, they will learn a different pattern of relationships and time investment. When they see you go to worship one day a week and value something as holy, both the pattern and the value will be permanently imbedded in their lives. They will see that investing time is wise, and they will follow suit.

Commandment 5: Respect your mom and your dad. ("Honor thy mother and thy father.")

Sometimes we think this commandment applies only if the parent is worthy of honor. But there are no terms and conditions attached to the command. We honor our parents because it is right, not because it is easy. We reap benefits from honoring them regardless of whether they deserve it. As parents, the best way we can teach our kids to respect our authority is to show them how much we respect our own moms and dads. When we listen to our parents' opinions, meet their needs, and speak highly of them, our children will see the value of respect.

Not only does honor create peace in the home, but it also teaches kids to have respect for all those in authority. In learning to honor Mom and Dad, kids develop the character to honor their pastor, priest, or rabbi, their teachers and principal, police officers, government officials, and public speakers. The ability to demonstrate honor begins in the home, but it applies everywhere. Ted says this is one reason he enjoys teaching his kids honor—he knows it is easier for him to teach it to them than to have them learn it in the back of a police car:

> Most of the time my three youngest boys are respectful toward their mother, but every once in a while I will hear one of them be disrespectful toward Gayle. Usually that happens when I'm at home in my study or in the bedroom, and they are unaware that anyone is listening. But soon they hear Dad's voice coming from upstairs or around the corner: "Boys, don't treat your mother that way!" Gayle can handle these guys and doesn't need me to defend her. But Gayle and I know there is a difference between Mom's voice and Dad's voice, and we believe that boys need to know how to respond to both. When my voice comes down the staircase demanding honor toward their mother, there is always quick compliance, which is going to keep me, in later years, from having to deal with the school system, the police department, or a warden. The lesson of respect for authority is learned in honoring Mom and Dad.

Commandment 6: Value people.
("Thou shalt not murder.")

In the last chapter, we discussed the importance and influence of entertainment. If there is one area that has been affected by entertainment more than any other, it is the devaluation of people. In most popular television shows, movies, and songs, women are sex objects (often of their own choosing), and men are either gunslinging imbeciles or emasculated wimps. People are little more than machines or tools for other people's purposes. For this reason, and in remembrance of the sixth commandment, we need to remember the lesson from the last chapter: help your kids with their entertainment choices. Be directional, intentional, and wise. Use your intuition. Don't let their audio/visual input ruin your work as a parent. We can teach our children the value of life, but watching 200,000 acts of violence by the age of sixteen is going to undo that value.[4] And once the value of life is gone, other people become disposable. They may only exist with our permission, and then we have the foundations for a society that uses people for the good of the state rather than one that uses the power of the state as a service to people. Abortion, euthanasia, suicide, violence, abuse, and hatred take over when people don't value people.

Of course, devaluing people takes on all kinds of more subtle forms, some of which can be just as destructive. We've all enjoyed dinnertime conversation as our teenagers tell us about the "other groups" at school. As young people grow up and begin to assimilate with particular groups within their school, neighborhood, or church, they sometimes learn the adolescent art of putting others down. You've heard it before. The snowboarders think the skiers are inferior. The chess clubbers think the jocks have no brains. The cheerleaders think the skateboarders are weird. They laugh and joke as they walk across the living room acting out the people they don't like. Some of this is innocent fun, but some of it results in the type of cliquish hatred we saw at Columbine. And if nothing else, Columbine and the other school shootings have reminded us that life is valuable, making this commandment more applicable than ever. As parents, we can help our kids appreciate the uniqueness of those around them. We don't need to be prudes, nor do we want to lose our sense of humor, but we don't want to sow the seeds of hatred or superiority that breed disrespect for others. Remember that your teens are waiting to see how you'll respond to others to determine the way they'll respond to others.

Commandment 7: Discipline your sexuality.
("Thou shalt not commit adultery.")

Everyone is sexual, but according to the Bible, human sexuality is not just for mating. In addition to reproduction, our sexuality is for intimacy, pleasure, defense against temptation, and comfort. Because of these things, human sexuality has a more complex role and meaning. For Jewish and Christian believers, sex is holy because it is reflective of a covenant relationship. That's one reason why people feel betrayed when their partner is sexual with someone else. This isn't true among rabbits and cows, but it is among people. For our children to enjoy quality, satisfying sexual activity as adults, they have to understand the value of disciplined sexuality.

Most people are biologically able to mate at or before thirteen years of age, but most are not ready for marriage until they are twenty-one or twenty-two. The adolescent years are difficult partly because teens are physiologically prepared for sex, but they are not ready for the responsibilities of having children, nor do they have the wisdom for long-lasting commitments to another person. Adolescence is the perfect time for all of us to learn the value of controlled sexuality. Unfortunately, our society is making a mistake by assuming that kids have to be active with one another and is, in a sense, teaching them that because they are animals, they can't control themselves. This is a setup for failed marriages, heartbroken relationships, and harsh abuses like rape, incest, and other sexual crimes that damage individuals and families and place a burden on all of society.

But because God told us not to commit adultery, we know sexual behaviors can be controlled and disciplined. Mature people testify, practically universally, that those with the most satisfying sex lives are those who are in monogamous heterosexual relationships. Sexual morality and satisfaction hinges on sexual discipline, so for our children to have great marriages, great sex lives, and great families, they have to learn from us the value of sexual discipline.

Commandment 8: Earn your own way.
("Thou shalt not steal.")

Most of us can still remember the endless "when I was your age" talks when we were young. Remember enduring story after story as your dad or granddad would embellish the values of "the good old days"? Woven into those stories always was the common thread of hard work. Our dads and granddads weren't trying to bore us—they were trying to teach us to appreciate hard work. Work makes us respect one another's possessions because it teaches us that those possessions are the rightful reward of the worker. When we work, we learn that other people have worked for their own "stuff," and we have worked for ours too.

If our teens hear us whining about other people's cars, clothes, and homes, they will get the idea that other people have things that should belong to us. They will never be able to give to others because they will be too busy finding ways to get more things or despairing about all the things they cannot have. Knowing that we can think, work, and earn the things we need and want is one of the greatest privileges of our society. The people who made America great are those who didn't depend on others to get things done or to provide things for them but went out and created opportunity and earned their way. These people live with a clean conscience, laugh easily, and sleep well. But those who steal from others, or simply depend upon others to care for them, develop a dark side of dissatisfaction and dependence. They are never satisfied, they never get enough, they are never content. We think parents should give generously to their children, but we don't think children should expect others to give to them. Children should expect to earn their way, and be grateful when they don't have to.

Commandment 9: Tell the truth.
("Thou shalt not bear false witness.")

There are two creeping deceptions in popular culture today. The first is that there is no such thing as truth. This is a horrible misunderstanding. In fact, it is a philosophical contradiction—"Absolutely nothing is absolutely true." Some facts are established. Some things work, others don't. Some things are right, others are wrong. We know for certain that love is better than hate, that faithfulness is better than betrayal, and that Pepsi is better than Coke (well, maybe there is room for debate on that last one). There is truth in this life, and it is up to us to find it.

The second deception is that we should always do whatever is necessary to promote our personal good, even if it means lying, or, to use the more popular term, "spinning." But God, in the ninth commandment, is saying that we need to avoid deception and trust truth. He is saying that it is always better to be honest than dishonest. He's establishing a plumb line of truth for our lives.

Our criminal justice system is struggling right now because of the assault on big ideas of truth and justice. Lawyers don't hesitate to misrepresent facts, and judges often are forced to make rulings that are legally correct but don't serve justice, truth, honor, or the common good. Witnesses regularly can be manipulated to testify for their own good rather than to just state the facts. Words don't mean what they are supposed to mean, and facts aren't clearly established in an adversarial world that values self more than truth. The results of this assault reach far beyond the courtroom: marriages don't last, friendships break down, churches stop serving, and police stop protecting when the line between truth and lie is blurred.

Lying erodes everything that is good. When people become deceptive, our justice system, our legislature, our manufacturing plants, our schools, and our homes all stop working efficiently. Grocery stores can't function when people are deceptive. Buying a plane ticket, a car, or a hamburger becomes very complex when people are dishonest. Nothing works when people are deceptive. Thomas Huxley said that truth is "the heart of morality." It is also the heart of peace, and of great, successful lives. From an early age, our children must know the value of truth. Make truth a highly valued commodity in your family. Seek the truth. Tell the truth. Live with truth. Trust truth.

Commandment 10: Be grateful for what you have. ("Thou shalt not covet.")

Several years ago, a close friend of ours, Brandon, was denied an insurance policy due to blood test results that had indicated liver disease. For two weeks, Brandon thought he had contracted a terminal illness, and he and his family lived in dread and sorrow. He began to make arrangements for his family, and he spoke with us about all the people and things he would miss. "I lost so much time worrying about what I didn't have," he said, "that I neglected to appreciate what I did have." After two weeks, the insurance company called with an apology: they had confused their blood samples. Brandon was healthy.

Brandon's experience reminded all of us that every day is a blessing. Every "good morning," every kiss, every hug, every glance at the sky, every mountain scene, every boat ride. With this mentality, the positive power of a grateful heart has come alive for both of us. We don't complain, we don't gamble. Instead, we build. We're grateful.

And that's character. Keeping your cool when your children disappoint you. Staying steady when things don't work out. Working hard for the good of your family. Living well, giving with a grateful heart, seeing people smile when they see you approaching. Seeing your kids smile when they see you because they love and trust you.

With these Ten Commandments firmly in hand, we can all be Michelangelo and find the beautiful sculpture in the middle of rough rock. These parameters are the best known and most proven tools we have for shaping character. They have worked for billions of people for thousands of years, and they can certainly work for our teenagers today.

CHAPTER
Six

Give Them Tools: Developing a Magnetic Personality

The first time you meet Winston [Churchill] you see all his faults, and the rest of your life you spend in discovering his virtues.

LADY CONSTANCE LYTTON

A survey was conducted recently to discover the average person's greatest fear. You'd probably think it was a fear of dying, heights, or confined places, but none of these ranked even in the top three. The number one fear that people have is—*public speaking*. That's right, speaking in front of a crowd evokes more butterflies and knotted guts then anything else. John will never forget his inaugural address at New Life Church:

It was my first time speaking in front of our five-thousand-member congregation. I remember waking that morning from a long night of countless nightmares about forgetting to wear clothes, slaughtering the English language, and suddenly losing my voice. I managed to get to church in time to pace nervously in the foyer and hold awkward conversations with people whose faces bled into a homogenous blur. As the service grew closer, I could feel the lining of my stomach growing tighter and tighter. It was as though there was some invisible force deep inside me trying to push itself out of my body. I felt like Captain Kirk in some bizarre episode of *Star Trek*. I heard my name from the platform as Ted introduced me to the church. I felt my legs carry me to the podium. My heart raced, then stopped, then raced again. My knees trembled. I broke into a cold sweat. But I kept moving . . . and speaking. The next forty-five minutes passed in an awkward combination of slow motion and fast-forward. I remember feeling like I was floating high above the crowd watching myself speak and desperately wishing I could grab the words that I saw spilling out of my mouth and cram them back inside. Time passed, I nearly passed out, and eventually I found myself sitting in Ted's office with my face in my hands and my tie hung loosely around my neck.

"I bombed," I sighed as Ted walked gingerly into his office. At first, he didn't say anything. He turned and closed the door behind him and took his place on his highback swivel chair. He paused, looked me in the eye, warmly grinned, and said, "That was fantastic." My eyes widened. My breath steadied.

"Really?"

"Yes, really," Ted said. And for the next thirty minutes Ted embarked on a journey of critique. His comments weren't about my ability to expound on Modern English derivatives of the Greek language. He said nothing about my skill at handling ancient texts. Instead, he talked about something that had hardly crossed my mind in the days approaching my sermon: personality. He talked about communicating with people by improving my posture, poise, and delivery. He painstakingly coached me to stand up tall, to speak with confidence, to look people in the eye, and to articulate with concise clarity. I couldn't believe it. He liked my message, but he knew I wouldn't be effective in delivering it to others unless I understood the principle of communication and connection by presenting myself well.

The next time John preached, he had as many notes in the margins of his sermon reminding him of posture and poise as he had actual sermon material. And it's been steady improvement both in people skills and in public speaking ever since. Why? Because, in that memorable conversation, we sidestepped the usual discussion on knowing the facts (knowing the facts should be a given) and focused on something more subtle but just as important: the sharpening of a personality.

In this chapter, we're going to attempt CPR on the lost art of personality. Hardly anyone teaches teens about personality anymore. When was the last time a fifteen-year-old called you "Sir" or "Ma'am"? That's because hardly any adults worry about that kind of respect anymore. When was the last time you called someone "Sir" or "Ma'am?" Such courtesies are part of personality, and personality is what makes people attractive. It is the difference between the old woman who growls at everyone who walks by and the old woman who smiles at everyone who walks by. It is the difference between the husband who ignores his wife except to snap at her and the husband who listens to his wife with respect. For a teen, it may mean the difference between success and failure.

We want to clarify that we're not saying that an empty person with a great personality can be successful and influential. Even though that does happen, we're not advocating that here. We're advocating that our teens develop strength in character and depth of insight by living life well in our homes, and then communicate those qualities outside of the home through a dynamic personality. So one of our responsibilities as parents is to develop a magnetic personality in our kids.

But how do we do it? What are the elements of personality that are critical for a successful, happy twenty-first-century teen?

THE ART OF CONVERSATION

Have you ever had one of these phone calls?

"Hello?" No answer. "HELLO?"

"Hello?" comes the loud but lazy response. "Uh, today we are offering . . . ," and the person on the other end begins reading their opening sales paragraph in a dry, tired monotone. You can barely tell what the telemarketer is saying much less selling. After the first paragraph, you interrupt to say you are happy with the current service. The salesperson then begins to blandly read the second paragraph, again slurring their speech together unintelligibly. Your assurances that you don't want to consider an alternative company don't end the call; even gladly giving the names of a few ornery people you know would be interested doesn't help. Finally, the telemarketer gets the picture, lazily slurs, "Okay," and hangs up.

What must this salesperson be like? They are trying to earn a living, which is admirable. But it is apparent that no one has ever coached them on how to speak on a telephone, how to articulate clearly, or how to connect with others. They are at a disadvantage. Their sales numbers are probably going to be below average, and they will soon be dismissed. From one phone conversation, they have depicted themselves as lazy, poorly trained, and incompetent. Very few people would want to buy from them, and they would never understand why. The telemarketer would probably blame the product or a supervisor, or complain that they were assigned the wrong customers. But those things are not to blame—it's their training, it's their presentation, it's their personality, it's them.

Strong communication skills are a key to success. If you know how to speak, and choose to use lazy speech for effect, that's fine. But if you are trapped in lousy speech, you're in trouble.

We coach our kids on the art of conversation frequently. Actually, we hardly ever address it specifically unless an opportunity presents itself, but we model quality conversation every day. By the time our children get into their mid-teens, they have confidence talking with anyone and understand the difference between a conversation with their buddies and their teacher, their grandfather and the neighbor across the street. A lot of these differences are subtle and can only be learned with practice, and of course we must give due adherence to the unspoken cultural rules in various communities, regions, and individual families. But in general, there are five basic tips that will help any teen or adult learn the art of conversation:

1. Stand Up Straight, Look Them in the Eye, and Smile

We all enjoy meeting young men or women who have the personal confidence to introduce themselves to an adult or other young person with assurance. Standing up straight rather than slouching and looking people in the eye with a warm, accepting smile is a significant entrée into the adult world. But young people don't know how to do it unless we teach them. A small percentage—a very small percentage—will do it naturally, but most need coaching. They can't be shamed into it or embarrassed publicly into doing it. Teenagers want to be able to be proud of their parents when they are with them and be willing to be coached.

Granted, in some cultures people don't greet one another this way, and we need to adjust accordingly. But in most Western civilizations, a warm, confident greeting communicates acceptance and responsibility, which is a must to catch the attention and receive the respect of adults.

2. Respond with Confidence—Don't Mutter

Choir, drama, public competitions, and athletics all help young people project confidence by opening their mouths to speak clearly. When we meet a young person who has the confidence to speak to us clearly with sparkling eyes and a warm grin, we immediately connect with these young people. Model for your teen the ability to speak out loud instead of muttering into your shirt.

3. Learn People's Names, and Use Them Properly

It has been said that there is nothing more beautiful for anyone to hear than the sound of his or her own name. Learning to use people's names with respect and courtesy is fundamental to basic conversation. This simple act will not only endear people but it will help to create in your teenager a sense of respect and thoughtfulness that will be the seeds of a magnetic personality. Kids (and, indeed, every one of us) must not only remember people's names but also learn to use them with the proper titles. An elder or someone who has earned a significant title should always be addressed by their formal title unless permission has been granted otherwise. It is "Uncle Lance," not "Lance." It is "Mr. Elliott," not "Bruce"—and certainly not, "Hey you!" This might seem stuffy or insincere, but really it's simply common courtesy and demonstrates thoughtfulness rather than bootlicking. Learning to use people's names with the proper titles will help your teen connect with people, be respected by people, and will directly help your teen know where they fit in relationship with other people. If remembering people's names is difficult, there are lots of resources available for memory improvement, such as *Don't Forget: Easy Exercises for Better Memory* by Danielle C. Lapp.

4. Develop a General Knowledge Base

Versatility in conversation is invaluable. Strong conversationalists aren't experts on every subject, but they are relatively informed and well-read. During Thomas Jefferson's term as president, he was known for hosting frequent dinner parties centered around the art of conversation. In Jefferson's social circle, it was generally accepted that the ability to carry on lucid conversation was paramount to any public achievement. Historian Stephen Ambrose, in his book *Undaunted Courage,* notes that discussions at the White House varied from natural science to philosophy, from geography to Indian affairs, from athletics to politics. Whether your teens aspire to become a president, professor, or pastor, the ability to converse over a broad range of subjects will help them step from the lobby of the average to the mezzanine of the elite. As Jefferson proved, a general knowledge base is essential to engaging conversation. Today we have become accustomed to surface conversations that neither engage us mentally nor stimulate us proactively. Encourage your teen to grasp a general understanding of politics, entertainment, sports, and religion, and you'll be amazed at the depth of conversation and friendships that will emerge. You're teen doesn't have to be an Einstein, but a basic information base will help him or her become a confident teen and potential leader.

5. Focus on the Other Person

Many people fail at conversation simply because they are too interested in fronting their own point of view. They don't want to talk to someone—they want to talk *at* someone. Help your teen to learn to listen in their conversations (again, the best way to teach them this lesson is to do it yourself). As they listen, they can gather information about the other person: his or her likes and dislikes, tastes and interests. They can make mental notes, remember key expressions, and assimilate the most important information about that person's life. This information can then be used as fodder for future talks. A good rule of thumb is the "Twenty-Five-Percent Rule." The general idea here is to tell only twenty-five percent of what you know about a subject, allowing the other person to tell their point of view. Often, we are so anxious to let the other person know that "we already knew that," we're the experts, or to tell a story that tops theirs, that we lose sight of the purpose of conversation ... building relationships. Relationships are built on mutual respect, admiration, trust, and genuine interest. The old saying applies here: "They don't care how much you know until they know how much you care."

THE ART OF PRESENTATION

Ever met the unpresentable boy? You know, the one who sloshes into your living room like he's got tar stuck to the bottom of his shoes. His head hangs so low that it is barely visible. Bravely, you attempt a meaningful conversation with him, but his only response is shrugged shoulders, drooping eyes, sideways glances, and yawns. If he gets real excited, maybe he'll slide his toe across the carpet or take his hands out of his pockets.

You recognize this boy. Maybe he's your daughter's boyfriend, maybe he's your next-door neighbor, or maybe he's your own son. In any case, this alien communication style is so common that it's comical. Many people say that this type of behavior is harmless and simply adolescent, but don't believe it. Once habits are formed, good or bad, innocent or intentional, they are hard to break. As you train your teenager in developing a magnetic personality, the art of presentation is just as important as the art of conversation.

Sociologists have proven that we learn twenty percent of what we hear and thirty percent of what we see. How we communicate with our body language is perhaps more important than what we communicate with our spoken words. As we mentioned, teach your teen as young as possible to greet people with a firm handshake. Not a vise grip, just a confident grasp. Teach them to look people in the eye when meeting them and talking to them. Teach them the importance of being presentable.

To return to the conversation discussion, a large part of any conversation is maintained by nonverbal signals. Focusing on the other person, which we mentioned above, is a nonverbal skill. If you're having a conversation in a crowded room or hallway, never look over the shoulder of the person you're addressing or look around the room while they are talking. Doing so communicates disinterest. If you are interested, look at them and engage them. If you are uninterested or need to go, graciously change the subject or excuse yourself. But in the process, stand up, look them in the eyes and engage them. It takes guts and a willingness to connect with others, but the rewards far outweigh the price.

For teens, this advice is priceless. Where today are our teens learning good nonverbal skills? Where are they learning to have a crisp but warm personal appearance? While your teens are still at home, take the opportunity to encourage them to appreciate the nonverbal aspects of a magnetic personality. You don't have to throw out the baggy jeans and sandals—just help them enjoy learning the advantages of good personal presentation.

THE ART OF PRESERVATION

Around our organization we've developed a basic theory that it takes four years to really get to know someone. Four years seems pretty accurate. You can wear masks for a while, but after four years, the game of masquerade is hard to play. Time and experience cements a relationship, taking it past surface formalities and into that rare thing we call "friendship." Friendship isn't a cheap, easy-come-easy-go fraternal association; it is a genuine, life-giving experience that is sometimes humiliating, sometimes comforting, and always enduring. True friendship can only be formed through breaching another person's life and connecting with that person. The arts of conversation and presentation are essential ingredients in the initial path toward friendship, and once a relationship begins to form, it can be maintained through the art of preservation.

Preserving a friendship is an art for one simple reason: friendships are a funny breed. At times, friendships are as easy as Tom Sawyer and Huckleberry Finn sitting on the bank of the Mississippi, watching the riverboats float by, laughing at squirrels, and waiting for their fishing lines to jump. But with one weird look, small miscommunication, or bad mood, friendships can suddenly become a lot like the fish at the other end of those lines: slippery, feisty, and frustrating. Learning to handle the slippery fish takes patience, commitment, and love, and some people, sadly, never learn. The teenage years are often some of the most frustrating years to try to develop friendships, because being cool is more important than being sincere and being popular is more important than being friendly. This may not be true for your teen, but it is true for many teens, leaving many teenagers lonely and unpracticed in the art of preservation—an art they will value highly in the years to come.

While your teens are still at home, you have a prime opportunity to help them learn how to develop genuine friendships—the type of friendships that will impact them the rest of their lives. Once again, the best way to teach this art is through modeling. If you really want your teens to have close friends, your family needs to have close friends. We have structured our lives so that our kids can immediately see the benefit of good friends. We have made a choice to live in one place, go to one church, and keep long-term relationships. As our kids grow up, they will remember Dad playing basketball with his buddies every summer. They'll remember Mom and her best friend staying up late talking over cups of tea in the kitchen. They'll recall knowing the same people all their lives, and those memories will instill in them the value of close friendships.

With this in mind, we advise families to live in one community for as long as possible. We know that this isn't always possible as in the cases of military families or changing job opportunities, but if the choice is between a slightly higher salary or the chance to remain in one community, choose the latter. Children who grow up in one school system have a great opportunity to learn how to preserve relationships. And in most cases, kids get a sense of security from knowing that their teacher knew their older brother or sister. Also, staying in one community allows the parents of two teenage friends to know one another. It is a remarkable strength for teens to know that the people they talk to will be talking to other people who know their parents and their parents' friends.

Again, we're not saying that people should rigidly stay in one place and never adjust their relationships. And in some cases, intertwined relationships like we've described can become negative and counterproductive. But when families help one another grow through stages in life, and when communities acknowledge the importance of helping one another, then communities begin producing great kids, great leaders, and great thinkers.

Another key to preserving relationships is empathy. In all of our friendships, we must learn to hurt when friends hurt and celebrate when friends triumph. When frustration is their *modus operandi,* we help them find solutions because we feel how they feel. Being empathetic is really just being thoughtful. It is listening, remembering, thinking about a friend's needs. It is a phone call in the middle of the day. It is an invitation to lunch on any given week. It is a willingness to "do" life with them. If your teens see you treating your friends with empathy and true concern, they are certain to follow in suit.

Preserving friendships is always easier and more rewarding if each friend is encouraging the other to be a better person. Don't enable your friends to live life poorly. Develop an air of camaraderie where you and your friends help each other strive to live great lives. As you do this, your teen will learn that a fundamental aspect of all good friendships is the promotion of the other's good. Then, you can trust that your teen will choose to befriend the type of people who help them make positive choices.

Maintain open conversations with your teen about friendships—both yours and theirs. John remembers the countless times his parents would take long walks with him to talk about life, school, and friends. Like most teens, he'd often think to himself "you don't know my friends" when the conversation turned to his choice of companions. He remembers the times his parents warned him against certain friends and coached him on how to establish better relationships with others. He remembers how during his high school years the conversations would often turn to his choice of girlfriends. At the time, he didn't necessarily always value the advice given, but now happily married and working with great friends, he's really grateful for the guidance and advice.

Both of us remember watching our parents enjoy each other and value close friendships. If your kids are constantly hearing and seeing that you value intimacy, they will value it too. There are a thousand subtle tricks to having good friendships, and you've learned most of them simply by living a number of years. Your teen will benefit enormously from watching you in your friendships. Preserving relationships is a skill, an art. It's an art worth developing.

The World Is Waiting

The dominant theme here is to model a good life for your teen. If you have a magnetic personality, your teen will want to develop one too. So chase after that intangible thing that attracts people to you—personality. Take a good, hard look at your own personality and decide today to make it better. Determine to really like people. Remember that everyone has a story and it's our job to discover their stories and help them write new chapters. Discover the joys in life, and live for those joys. Don't be consumed with money and clothes and professional attainments—be consumed with people.

Think of this: Every day, great men and women from all walks of life leave this earth and step into eternity. Think of the great men and women of history who have left incredible legacies behind. The Apostle Paul, Martin Luther King Jr., Winston Churchill, Abraham Lincoln, Mother Teresa, C. S. Lewis, King David—to name a few. Who will dare to fill their shoes? Who will dare to step into their lives and adopt their personal magnetism?

The world is waiting for you. The world is waiting for those daring few who will grab hold of the coattails of life and never let go. Those chosen few who will stand up tall, look life in the face, and march down the sunny side of the street. The world is waiting for those chosen few who will determine to live a life that attracts others and leads them toward greatness. We dare you to be one of the chosen few. We dare you to build your teenager to be one of the chosen few. Will you change history? Will you write history? Believe it or not, it begins with a quick step, a bright eye, and a sure smile. Try it.

PART
Three

Four Collateral
Strengths

CHAPTER
Seven

Family: Life at the Kitchen Table

There is nothing like staying at home for real comfort.

JANE AUSTEN

As we begin this chapter, we need to let you know that we, the authors, are having a bit of a fight. Well, maybe not a fight, but at least a debate. A friendly contest. We suppose you could call it a "Story Tell-Off." You see, we're both convinced that we've experienced the greatest family dinnertime episodes of all time, and this is our chance to see what each other is made of....

John:
    Mom used to lean out of the kitchen window and call us to dinner in that unmistakable vocal pitch that only mothers possess. I remember running into the kitchen along with my five noisy brothers and sisters, competing to be the first to discover what was for dinner. As we stormed in, the kitchen

became a jungle of sounds and smells. Somehow Mom managed to skillfully dodge a soccer ball, listen to a violin recital, and stir the macaroni all at the same time (which I now realize is superhuman, as I can barely cook the macaroni alone).

The kitchen would become a gymnasium as we instinctively divided the dinner chores, each person doing their part to set the table. One filled the glasses, another organized silverware, and another "tested" the evening meal (that wasn't an official responsibility—I just thought it needed to be done). The din in the kitchen would reach the decibel level of a Rolling Stones concert and keep growing until Dad walked into the room, and then it would become even louder. After hugs, I-love-yous, and inside jokes, we'd gather around the table for the one quiet moment of supper time: Dad praying for our meal and thanking God for the day.

I'll always remember those prayers. There seemed to be something extra special about those moments with the eight of us, hand-in-hand around the table in a bona fide family circle. Our personalities were unique, but our hearts were connected. As I sit here now, those mental snapshots are so priceless: snapshots of Mom and Dad navigating six kids through life; snapshots of Dad serving potatoes with a French accent (no, he wasn't French). Happy glances. Spilled milk. Flying green beans. Hidden broccoli. Laughter. Life. Family. I remember. How could I ever forget?

Ted:

Sunday dinner after church was one of the special events no one in my family was allowed to miss. Some of my most vivid memories from childhood are those dinners: Dad stretched back in his chair laughing while we waited for the inevitable "table slap" that would send glasses of milk spilling onto the floor; Mom admiringly paying us her undivided attention as we kids told stories, acting out the mannerisms of our awkward teachers and crazy friends, embellishing every word. Dinner was a scene of home cooking, dinner guests, loud conversations, raucous storytelling, and Mom and Dad in love. We loved it.

Mom and Dad are both gone now, and each of my brothers and sisters have their own families. But my own family still follows Mom and Dad's example. We don't have the same consistency as my parents, but we guard our dinnertime after Sunday church and are able to have three or four evening meals together every week.

Recently, during one of these evening meals, the significance of the dinner table scene dawned upon me. At the opposite end of the kitchen table, alongside bowls of steaming potatoes and chicken casserole, sat my wife of over twenty years. Between us, lined up like a basketball team, were our five energetic children: two teenagers and three elementary school kids. Amidst the roar of laughing, storytelling, requests for someone to pass this or that, and kids getting up and sitting down, I could see that the values my mom and dad held were now in my own family.

As Jonathan, our handicapped son, was trying to tell a story, I pulled myself up across the length of the table, held myself above the glasses of milk in a push-up position, and kissed my wife. While I held myself in this awkward position, the younger kids giggled and the older ones shouted, as Gayle, their mother, kissed me good and long, right on the lips. The kids laughed as they helped me get back to my seat without falling into the food. The grins on their faces told me what they were thinking: "Mommy and Daddy love each other, and they like each other too."

We're convinced that one of the foundations for great kids is a family that likes each other. As a family, we sacrifice for each other. We talk late into the night and make each other laugh and cry. We fight and heal, work together to clean up the garage and mow the yard, and live a routine life of dishes and yards and dirty bedrooms. This is our life, amazingly enough, formed at a dinged kitchen table.

As we paint pictures of families laughing, eating, and playing together, some of you may feel a knot deep down in your stomach. "Laugh together? Play together? I'd be happy if we could just talk to each other." Don't worry, you're not alone. As our kids grow up from bubbly little boys and girls who ask a hundred questions into cool teenagers who answer in grunts and glances, we all go through difficult stages when successful parenthood seems like a distant dream.

But it is during those same stages when it is vitally important for us, as parents, to dig our heels in deep, set our faces straight, and determine to be the best parents we can possibly be. And without a doubt, we can truly be magnificent parents, no matter what the circumstance. So put on your warm-ups, stretch your muscles, and get ready to jump into the game. This is the game of life, and these are some of the most exciting minutes of the match.

The junior high and high school years form and shape kids unlike any other time in their lives. The days ahead are some of the scariest, most thrilling, and challenging days our teens will ever experience. They are years full of finals, fears, and firsts. The first car, the first crash, the first crush, the first kiss. In these years, our kids begin to develop their individual interests, hobbies, and talents. During these years, teens explore and experiment and define who they are. And you're right in the middle of the game. In fact, you're the most important player in it. Really—in your teen's life, you're the most valuable player. You, more than anyone else, have the opportunity and privilege to mold them into great kids.

Of course, if you can't get through to them, you can't very well coach them. Understanding that the thought of talking with your teen might make you break out in a cold sweat, we want to give you a few practical tips that will make your journey of family-building a little easier. Here's a simple five-point parenting manual. Think of it as Berlitz for parents. We'll call it the Five Secrets of Building a Family.

SECRET 1: CARE ABOUT WHAT MATTERS TO THEM

You don't have get your eyebrow pierced or know the lyrics to the latest 'N Sync song to convince your teen that you care about her. All teenagers need is the assurance that you have taken notice of their lives, that you have made a special effort to take interest in the things that matter to them. What are their hobbies and interests? Make their interests your interests. This means not only asking them about soccer practice and choir, but also about the guy in Biology class. The feelings of a fifteen-year-old girl are just as valid as the feelings of a twenty-five-year-old woman. It is easy for us to undervalue our kids' relationship experiences, but remember that the things that we consider minor issues in a teenager's life can be their primary concern. Should you care? Of course you should care. It if matters to them, make it matter to you. Often, our job as parents is simply to be there for our kids, ready to listen and understand.

SECRET 2: EMBRACE MOMENTS OF PERSONAL PAIN

Remember your first crush? Remember the pain of realizing that he or she didn't even know you were alive? Recalling those experiences is another key to communicating well with your teenager. Most of the time, heartbreak in a teenager's life seems pretty trite to us. But when painful times hit, it's an open door for you to build trust and respect with your teenager. A painful breakup, stinging failure, or devastating loss may be one of the few times a teenager's heart is open wide enough to let you in. Never miss out on an opportunity to coach your teen through a time of personal pain. As your teen gives you access to his or her heart during a time of crisis, guard it like a treasure. Avoid making them feel stupid or immature for hurting over something you might consider trite. Remember that their emotions and feelings are real and valid. (Also, realize that sometimes when you go out on a limb to get into your teenager's life, you might get rejected. That's okay—it's all part of the process.)

SECRET 3: PREPARE TO BE TAKEN FOR GRANTED — IT IS WELL WORTH IT

It goes without saying that raising children seems a thankless job at times. The task of making boys and girls into men and women is not for the feeble at heart. Accept the fact that raising kids means long days and sleepless nights with rare instances of gratitude. Don't expect to hear your teen say, "Oh, Mother Dearest, you are so wonderful! May I bask in the light of your superior wisdom?" Fat chance. Ted says that he didn't even realize his parents were real people until he was twenty-one. This responsibility called "parenting" is a bloody, sweaty, and tear-filled job, but take faith that it is also the greatest job on earth. You may never know the true difference that you made in your teenager's life until much later in your lifetime, but don't give up. Your ability to stick with it will determine your success or failure as a parent.

SECRET 4: STAY STEADY

More than anything else, teenagers are looking for people who will go the distance with them. In a world where people dine and ditch, gas and go, marry and split, it's important that kids see us as consistent providers and protectors. Staying steady does more to create a legacy of success in our kids then all the books, tapes, and seminars in the world. They need you, Mom and Dad. They need you, pastor and counselor. They need you to pass the test of time and be there. Be there for Little League games. Be there for science fairs and annual plays. Be there when they get home from school. The security that a teenager gets from having confidence in the fact that Mom and Dad love them and that one of you will be waiting for them when they get home can mean the difference between raising confident young adults and raising Cain.

SECRET 5: PRACTICE MODELING

We've saved the most important secret for last. Whether we realize it or not, our kids are modeling their lives after ours. Count on it—they take note of everything we do and everything we say. They watch how we communicate, how we love, how we work, play, worship, and rest. Our kids watch intently how we live our lives, and they make important decisions for their own lives as a result. If this is true, then it follows that we should be careful to live honorable lives. In other words, we should live the life we want our kids to live.

One day as Ted was taking Christy and Marcus to their high school, a police officer stopped him and wrote a ticket for speeding. Although he was thinking that the officer should be out chasing real criminals, Ted constrained his emotions and tongue and was respectful to the officer. Afterward, as his kids were laughing, Ted explained that the officer was working to save lives and that he was grateful that the officer was there to stop them from speeding. Christy and Marcus grinned at each other.

Later that morning, Ted was driving Alex and Elliott, his younger sons, to their elementary school and was stopped again and given another ticket. He cooperated, laughed, and gave Alex and Elliot the same talk. When everyone got home from school that day and began telling stories about Daddy's speeding tickets, Ted saw his children forming their attitudes toward the police department and the penalty of driving too fast. If he would have been angry or tried to get out of the tickets, he would have taught his kids to disrespect authority, lie, and be duplicitous in dealing with officers. In one day, modeling taught the Haggard kids more about respecting authority than any lecture ever could have.

You can follow this same practice in dealing with your kids' schools, relationships, and participation within the faith community. We work along with our children's teachers to educate them. When our children have conflicts or problems with a teacher or some other authority, we coach them, but we don't get involved ourselves unless asked by that authority. We have family friends whom we have known for years, and our children know that friends are valuable for our entire family. These long-term friendships are why we try to live in the same community for years and maintain relationships that last a lifetime.

Modeling a well-lived life is vital communication to our children. We treat our parents and siblings with honor and respect so our children will see us honoring our elders. We've chosen to pray before meals, help in the kitchen, lower our standard of living so one parent could be home when the kids are home, stay married, and believe in God. We've chosen to have a family night once a week, to schedule our events around piano recitals, football games, and choir performances so our kids can see us enjoying their talents. We try to model caring for one another and covering for one another. It's worth it. It's a life well lived.

As we've noted, modeling can mean anything from reacting to a speeding ticket to talking gently to your spouse. Being mindful of the little specifics is extremely important, for virtually every action we make, every word we speak, has significance in our lives. We could write another book on which values should be invested into our families, but here we'll limit ourselves to two, both of which can be modeled with wonderful success.

THE VALUE OF TIME TOGETHER (FAMILY NIGHTS!)

We have both started the process of establishing a weekly family night in each of our families. This has been a process and it takes commitment to maintain, but when we're doing it regularly, it always produces results. Family nights are like exercise: when we have them, we wonder why we don't have them all the time. When something causes us to miss them, it's hard to get them started again.

Family nights evolve depending upon the age of the children and the goals everyone wants to achieve. We think of family night as our opportunity to establish the fragrance of our home and instill in our children a legacy. Sometimes we have a family meeting; other times we have a cookout or go to a movie. Family night in the Haggard home is always an adventure:

We've gone through cycles where the children can each choose what we'll do on a given week, and we can count on it—Jonathan schedules a camp out, Alex wants to shut off the lights and play flashlight hide-and-go-seek. Sometimes family night is for all of us to go hear one of Marcus's performances in his high school band. When it's my turn or Gayle's turn, we want to work on the family mission statement or talk about the kids hating and hitting one another all the time.

But this is the time when communication is established, and all five of our kids, whether they are whining or rejoicing, love family night. How do I know? Because I'm their dad and I know, that's how. It's family night where family theme, purpose, chore assignment readjustments, vacations, schedules, and other family connections are established. Family night makes the rest of the week work, it makes the tone in the house remain civil (or I should say it gives us a guide to civility—It doesn't actually create it because we're raising teens).

In a world of drive-through restaurants, instant coffee, and remote controls, it's easy to think that we can raise a healthy family with little effort. The truth is, there is no such thing as an instant family. It takes purpose, patience, and most importantly, time together. If this is your pursuit, your children will follow suit.

THE VALUE OF WISDOM IN AGE

One reason the family structure is so important is that it gives a younger generation an opportunity to learn values from an older, mature generation. Unfortunately, our culture downplays the importance of the wisdom that comes with age; we're fighting an uphill battle to model the value of older people. But helping our kids to understand the value of long talks with grandma and grandpa will ensure that teenagers will hear proven answers to life's many questions. John grew up thinking of his grandparents as a second set of parents:

As far back as I can remember, my grandparents were a part of my life. They never drew attention because they never needed to. Mamu and Papu. They were my grandparents. They had moved to America in 1950 after escaping from Communist Latvia during World War II and eventually settled in Omaha. The war was over for Latvia, and now life began for my grandparents. Papu was determined to start over again and built a house in the middle of an empty field. More than twenty years later, my parents bought the house next door. We lived in the big white house next door to my grandparents during all of my childhood.

Every day after school, I remember running to Mamu and Papu's house to play, talk, and eat. But I never really realized the difference they made in my life until a few months ago. I was visiting my mother on my way to a business meeting in Michigan and had agreed to stop through Omaha on my way to Detroit. As always, I enjoyed my time with Mom, and as always, she insisted that I tramp next door to my grandparents' house to say "Hello." As I walked across the green lawn that connects my parents' house to my grandparents' house, my mind began to play back a million pictures from my childhood. I walked into the house just like I had thousands of times over the past twenty-nine years. But this time my grandmother didn't come running to the door like she used to. This time she called to me from one of the back rooms of the house. As I walked through the house, a thousand more memories blurred in my mind. Easters, Christmases, Thanksgivings. As I snapped out of my dazed trip down memory lane, I found myself sitting next to my grandfather, who was lying on his bed watching CNN. As I leaned down to give him a hug, I was surprised to remember the familiar smell of his cologne.

My mind raced once more to countless memories, this time solely of my grandfather. I remembered the Saturday mornings upheld as our tradition of fishing together, talking together, and eating ice cream together. Now, it was a struggle for him to make his daily trip to the YMCA to swim. I never thought of my grandparents as getting older. To me, they were forever young. Now, suddenly, it hit me like a ton of bricks. I realized that one day I would lose them, and I realized how much they had impacted my life. I looked deep into my grandfather's eyes and thought to myself, I want to be just like you. I looked up at Mamu, and she just smiled. She knew exactly what I was thinking. And that's what grandmas and grandpas do. They help us live. They teach us to love always, to forgive easily, to grow old gracefully.

Of course, some of us can't do this because our families are separated, and that is where being connected to a good church can help. But there are a number of creative ways to show kids the wisdom that comes with age. You can always make sure kids have older friends around the house to model various stages of life. Our church is located near the Air Force Academy, so our families have been fortunate to know some outstanding cadets who could serve as models for the next stage of life for our kids. As children grow older, you can make friends with slightly older people—inviting them to family outings and social events. This way, the next stage of life is not a mystery to children. They will admire these family friends and mimic their lifestyles.

In fact, that is one of the reasons we are writing this book together. Ted's kids look at John and Sarah Bolin as examples of what people are like when they grow up. As our families hang out together, Ted knows his kids are clueing in to details about John and Sarah's lives—listening to the things they talk about, noticing the types of decisions they make—and, in their admiration of the Bolins, discovering how to live. Like the Haggard kids look to John and Sarah to help them decide how to live, John and Sarah watch Ted and Gayle as examples of what they can become.

All adults know that older people help us live successfully, but teens won't learn the value of learning from older people unless we model it for them. In the old days, before socialized medicine and nursing homes, children, parents, and grandparents often lived in the same home or at least on the same property. Having multiple generations and people at different ages somehow inadvertently taught a generation of people what it meant to grow old, respect authority, and work hard. Today, we've drifted from the fact that it requires a community of family to raise a child, and it may be time that we bring it back. Kids need to watch Dad talk to his dad. Kids need to watch Mom and Dad and Grandma and Grandpa and their friends live life. Our kids will strive to be like our families as long as our families are safe places, full of destiny, hope, and, most importantly, love.

CHAPTER
Eight

Government: Order and Protection

When the freedom they wished for most was the freedom from responsibility, then Athens ceased to be free and never was free again.

EDITH HAMILTON

The sounds of Yanni ring inside the cockpit of your SUV. As the melody floats across your mind, every muscle in your body is soothed. An overwhelming sense of calm settles on you and you feel free. Suddenly, the lovely music is replaced with rude and familiar sirens. You're jerked out of your utopian dream and thrown sharply into a horrifying reality. It is the recurring nightmare of your adult life. Your stomach churns in knots and your eyes roll with disbelief. In your rearview mirror you see it clearly—your nemesis inching closer and closer toward your tailgate, taunting you like a pirate from some ancient fairy tale. The urge to run is quieted by a nudge of your conscience. You are trapped. Literally. You knew this busy intersection, with its steady diet of reckless and impatient drivers, was prey for traffic officers. And now you are the prey. At the tap on your window, you reach to grab your license and registration....

The eternal moments pass. You shove the speeding ticket into the glove box, and then the frustration sets in. After steaming the rest of the drive home, you burst into the house. You've already called your spouse from your cell phone, so the family is braced. Normally, your kids run and wrap themselves around your legs, but tonight they stay hidden in the den watching *Dawson's Creek*, listening cautiously for your reaction.

What do you say? How do you react? They're listening. They're watching. And they're assimilating.

One of the most neglected aspects of raising kids is building in them an understanding of and respect for government. Currently, it is more popular to satirize our government than to seek to understand the way our government tries to serve and protect us. But during our teenagers' formative years, while they are learning how to "do" life, it is imperative that we take advantage of the opportunity to help shape their opinions and convictions about government by modeling for them an appropriate response to social and political issues.

Both of our sets of parents told us that our government, although imperfect, was the best on earth. But they didn't explain why. Our parents explained that police officers were good people who could be relied on if help was ever needed, but they never talked about the real duty of protective government. Both of our parents believed that we live in a great country, but they never articulated why. Then, while we were working among the poverty-stricken in Asia, the contrast between different types of governments became real to us as we witnessed dictatorships, a public fear of the military, a corrupt police force, and public services that don't work. It happened again while we were in Africa—people starving on street corners while the police drove by in military vehicles, black markets, people scavenging for firewood and a little food. The difference? Culture? No. The difference is a combination of religion, politics, and economics. Great kids need a healthy understanding of the three and how they interface. In this chapter, we'll touch on politics and economics.

SETTLING THE ISSUES

We're writing this chapter at a coffee shop in downtown Colorado Springs. At the table across from us, a few college students are preparing for their final exams at Colorado College. In the last hour, we've noted that the conversations at their table have been as diverse as the students themselves. As we've eavesdropped, these bright young people have engaged in discussions about anything and everything (except their looming exams). The economy, the environment, gender issues, relationships, and, as you would expect, the educational system, have all been dissected with just the right amount of sarcasm.

As we watch them sip espresso and banter back and forth in friendly spite, we can't help but think of how valuable this process is. It's one of the things that makes America so great. In a public setting, we're all free to exchange ideas and form ideals, convictions, and worldviews. And as we sit here writing this book in the backdrop of this friendly and interesting exchange, we are all the more aware of how valuable your role as a parent and mentor is in this process.

Chances are, the underlying basis for these students' beliefs was formed not in the hallowed halls of a renowned school but in the well-worn hallways of a home. That's right: even the greatest minds of our world began to formulate an ideology of how the world should work as a son, daughter, brother, or sister, not as a pupil in the fourth row of Philosophy 101. Home is the place where we develop our basic ideological foundation. Home is where we discover who we are and who we want to become. During our turbulent teenage years, we develop a foundation of belief that teaches us to respect or disrespect authority, protect or neglect human rights, save or ruin the environment, and care for or disregard the poor.

As we discussed earlier, our kids will develop their lives largely according to the type of life that we model for them. Whether or not it is readily apparent to them or us, we can be sure that our kids are "watching" us. They are processing what they learn from the way we respond to life, and they are assimilating that information into their own worldview. "Stupid cops!" "That lying President!" "The thieving IRS!" It's all processed. The words you speak and the tone you use become unintended messages in the minds of our children. They're watching, learning, and deciding who they will become.

Sound like a lot of pressure? Trust us, you can handle it if you have settled the issues of life for yourself. If you haven't, parenting gives you an opportunity to do so. For better or worse, being a parent reveals everything about us. Children force all of us to peer deeply into our hearts, take personal inventories, and discover what is significant in life. Our children encourage us to mature, to make up our minds and come to a healthy resolve about what it means to be alive. If we don't, our children will mimic our actions and attitudes, which will frustrate us as we see ourselves in them. And that will hurt—especially when it comes to dealing with authority.

Training our kids how to respond to authority, especially government authority, is one of the most sobering and enlightening privileges we experience in life. Of course, we don't have to do it. We can always defer to the moviemakers, musicians, educators, and social workers to shape our kids. But why should we? While our children are still at home, we can make certain that they learn about government authority, thereby ensuring that they will be able to respond to a wide range of authority issues wisely later in life.

THE VALUE OF GOVERNMENT

As we've been writing this chapter, the coffee shop has filled with people wanting to load up with caffeine to survive the rest of the workday. A little while ago, a group of guys completely different from the students here this morning sat down at the table across from us. These guys, plainly enough, are jocks. Their conversation has been entertaining, ranging from girls and summer jobs to camping trips and the NBA playoffs. But eventually their talk landed on the inevitable: the Columbine High School shooting, where Eric Harris and Dylan Klebold were targeting athletes. They wondered aloud why the armed sheriff's deputy at the school ran from the shooters. They laughed eerily about the SWAT team members cowering behind busses in bulletproof vests while a teacher and students were dying inside. They mocked the rescue teams, pointing out that the students were the heroes, not the swat teams, police officers, or anyone else assigned to protect students. In true college form, they jokingly talked about the government that is here to "protect us."

"Sure," one of them said, "while those kids were trying to save each other, the government was waiting until it was safe. Our government is a joke. They have one standard for themselves and another for all of us."

A guy in baseball cap mentioned his psychology professor, who had lectured that morning on the rise of teen violence in public schools. As he explained how his professor believed that more state counselors were needed, one of the others interrupted with a loud, "Yeah, sure! Eric Harris was in therapy and was taking Luvox. That sure helped a lot!"

"C'mon," said another. "Kinkel from Oregon and Solomon from Georgia were both on Ritalin. Yep, that's the solution," he laughed. "More talk and more drugs. I'm sure the government would be happy to supply that—just so long as no one shoots at them!"

As we listen to these conversations, which are more frequent than ever, it is glaringly obvious that reactions to our government's authority can tend toward contempt. Admittedly, our government has cast a negative light upon itself as of late. While much of this has been mitigated, the fact remains that we need a government that serves the public, and we need citizens who will work to maintain a healthy, moral government. And while open discussion is one of our greatest protections from abusive government, it is imperative that discussion leads to specific civil action, not contempt.

As parents, it is our responsibility to train our kids to value good government and improve bad government. How? By depositing into their minds the principles that have made our lives successful and our society great. We must come to an understanding of the value of our government so we can pass it along to those we've been trusted to nurture.

WHAT WE TEACH OUR KIDS

We are persuaded that our children should have a working understanding of government before they can respect and honor government authority. So, through the years, in numerous conversations at the dinner table, at baseball games, on long drives and camping trips, we discuss the basics of government with our kids.

There are four contemporary resources we use to communicate these ideas—two movies and two books. *Saving Private Ryan* and *Braveheart* are both popular reviews of the roles of personal sacrifice and resistance of government tyranny. *The Greatest Generation* by Tom Brokaw and *The Book of Virtues* compiled by William J. Bennett both communicate values and ideals that form good government. All of these interesting resources can generate great conversation about governmental issues and, in our view, should be in every home.

We've seen some remarkable experiments with government in this century. We've read Marx and Engels, and some of the greatest thinkers in this century believed that communism was the answer to the evils of capitalism. Ideas like equal opportunity and the forced distribution of wealth, regardless of training and profession, sounded like utopia. Free medical care for all and the promise of full employment with food and housing for everyone excited people and made capitalism sound immoral, dark, and harsh. But as we all know, the promises of communism proved to be empty. Communism was a failure in government, leading to massive military dictatorships that ruthlessly took away individual liberties and evaporated private wealth.

Our constitutional republic, with the strength of free-market capitalism, took the opposite approach. Communism thought that if government worked to improve the common good, the lives of the individuals within the group would be improved. Capitalism, on the other hand, maintained that if government encouraged indi-viduals to improve themselves by providing goods and services to others, individual prosperity would cause the whole community to improve. In a constitutional republic like ours, where we are self-governed, free markets create wealth and the government serves the people. Innovation and creativity push the marketplace forward, producing an abundance of new goods and services—the prosper-ity that our kids take for granted, unless we teach them its value.

You might say to yourself, "Communism Smomunism. Why should I care? What I really want to know is how to get my sixteen-year-old son to stop talking back to me." But the way your teenager learns to respond to government authority will help determine how he will respond when you ask him to take out the trash. No doubt, young children will respond to authority simply because they want to make Mom and Dad happy and they want to avoid the wooden spoon, but teenagers need to understand *why* it's important to respond correctly to authority. Part of being a teenager is learning to question, critique, and react to authority. If a teenager under-stands how and why our government works the way it does, it will help them correctly determine how to respond to all types of authority.

Ironically, part of the challenge parents face in America is that we live in such a great political and economic environment. It is relatively easy to be an American because we are used to freedom. As church leaders, we've had the opportunity to travel all over the planet with teenagers and expose them to virtually every form of government and social structure in the world. We have taken teenagers into countries with governmental models of tyranny, communism, and monarchy, and exposed them to economic sys-tems that are dysfunctional at best. When we return home, these teenagers generally have a much higher level of respect for our elected governmental officials. When they get home, they respond with respect to police officers, are more interested in voting, and have a totally new insight into grocery stores that are stocked with food, consistent electricity, and phones that work.

If our teens can grasp a working understanding of how we govern ourselves, it will help them understand why they should respond with honor and respect. With a clear understanding of the role of government, our kids will begin to see elected officials not as tyrants or party-crashers but as servants.

GOVERNMENT OFFICIALS AS SERVANTS

In America, we elect our peers to govern us and call them "public servants." Their role is to serve, not to rule. No one wears any type of government uniform and carries a weapon unless they are under the authority of an elected civilian. That's why our police cars have signs painted on them reading, "To protect and to serve," and our military aircraft are available to carry sick children to hospitals.

This philosophy of government has produced an environment that allows the markets to create more wealth than the world has ever known. It provides the incentive to encourage even the poorest people to produce goods and services for others, at a profit, and gives a high percentage of our population greater wealth. Our small businesses produce more goods and services than any small businesses on earth. And our large, multi-national corporations deliver much of their profits to average hardworking people, their stockholders, their owners. When we allow free trade, people prosper. When we don't, we end up with either surpluses or shortages. Free markets automatically raise prices to stimulate production when we need more of something and naturally lower prices to discourage production when we have a surplus. Because of free markets, we have the right number of boxes of Captain Crunch and Honey Nut Cheerios on our grocery store shelves. And confounding those who believe that there should be a government central command to coordinate production on farms, the free market insures that apples are available year around.

America's fundamental ideas work. They are valuable. But along with modeling an appropriate response to government, how do we communicate these ideas to our children? How do we encourage our children to value them?

DEVELOPING A WORLDVIEW

As we've already mentioned, every other year our church sponsors short-term overseas mission trips. In these trips, teenagers travel throughout the world to minister to people in need. Right now we have teams preparing to go to Albania, Nepal, India, and several countries in Africa and Europe. In these countries, teens will experience a variety of spiritual climates and living conditions. They will see lush natural resources of other nations, while the people there are living in poverty. They will see "developed" nations that have poor electrical service and limited clean water. And on every trip, the inevitable questions will come: "How can we help these people? Why are they so poor? What will make their lives better?"

We encourage families and churches to travel as much as possible with teenagers in order to raise these questions and provide accurate answers. It's good for a teenager who is accustomed to a police department being available to serve citizens to visit a country where the police department controls and harasses its citizens. It's an enlightening experience to be in the airport of a free country where there is little or no military presence and then to visit a country with men armed with submachine guns to intimidate and control. The greatest way to learn about the impact of government policy and grow in appreciation of our government is to see the results of other government systems. Then life in America starts to make sense.

If you can't go overseas yourself, associate with a church or ministry that will provide these opportunities for your children. Our Declaration of Independence and constitution become valuable documents when your teen is having to sneak through the night in some Islamic or communist country to attend a Bible study, knowing that if they get caught people will be imprisoned for publicly reading a Bible. Suddenly, Lincoln and the Civil War make sense. The reasons for World War II, the Cold War, and the undeclared wars like Korea and Vietnam begin to become apparent.

Kids killing kids in a rich American school because their feelings were hurt when others made fun of them? It just doesn't make sense unless we understand the wickedness that grows in the human heart when we refuse to look beyond ourselves into the world at large. Without a doubt, it is worth it for parents of wayward children to sell their homes, cash in their retirement accounts, or downgrade their transportation, if it means they can help their kids. Ted often mentions that he wears the same sports blazer all the time so that he can take his kids on trips to help people in genuine need. We can afford to raise our children if it's our priority, but we must be willing to sacrifice.

These traveling experiences create an opportunity to settle issues every adolescent should face and answer questions that will make responding appropriately to a government easier to do. Discussing questions of government and economics with your teen will not only help in teaching them how to respond to authority, but it will make your dinner table and late night talks more interesting, engaging, and life changing. Here are a few questions you might want to begin with:

- What is the difference between a constitutional republic and other forms of government?
- How is wealth created?
- Why should elected civilians have authority over the military and the police?
- Who sets prices?
- Why do we have an independent judiciary?
- Is it bad to be wealthy?
- Are corporations bad?
- What is a publicly held corporation?
- Who gets the profits?
- Why is freedom of religion, expression, and association important?

When these questions are discussed sitting on a log in the middle of a mud hut village in some foreign country, the ideals of family, wealth, purpose, justice, and citizenship take on infinitely more meaning. The foreign setting fosters an opportunity to talk about being a free citizen and making our families, communities, and nation a better place to live. It's a time to talk about grandpa and grandma and the sacrifices they made in World War II. In this setting, the value of living for others is developed. If this can be taught while falling asleep in a mud hut, sitting around a cooking fire on an impoverished Indian reservation, or feeding starving people in a refugee camp, teenagers will learn. They will return home appreciative and ready to work in the soup kitchen, volunteer in a nursery, and assist the handicapped and the elderly. The world changes in our homes when our teens understand the world.

Several organizations exist to help our kids understand government and free markets. The Scouts, Junior Achievements, and other community service organizations provide great opportunities for our kids to learn about authority and entrepreneurial thinking. One of us, John, was an Eagle Scout, and the other, Ted, was an Explorer Scout, and both of us were able to develop small businesses and travel internationally when we were young. The opportunities for expanding our teen's worldview are out there if we'll pursue them.

THE RESPONSIBILITY OF CITIZENSHIP

Understanding how our government works and getting a global view of life will help your teen to appreciate his or her roots and culture. As a healthy respect for government is fostered, a sense of ownership begins to take place in regard to national heritage. The appreciation and value of national heritage is called citizenship. Citizenship is important, more important than a nice new car, a warm house, or a full stomach. Most of us think little of our citizenship, but it is vital for our kids to understand the meaning of being a member of a community that is working to make life better. That's what makes America great. John's grandparents, whose own worldview gave them a unique understanding of freedom, taught him to value citizenship by the way they lived everyday:

My grandparents have been in America for forty years. They adopted the United States as their residence in 1944, but this has never been their home. After five decades in America, Mamu and Papu still speak broken English, and they hardly live like well-off Americans. They can their own food, till their own garden, and save everything. He gardens and she saves. I still remember how every Christmas morning, Mamu would carefully fold the wrapping paper of every gift to reuse it another time. I'm sure today there's a box of wrapping paper in her basement that would qualify as an antique in itself.

They live this way because they remember. They remember World War II, the depression, and the terror of tyranny. They remember being ripped from their home in Latvia and shoved onto a train. They remember the fearful moment when they kissed each other good-bye at a train station in Germany, not knowing if they'd ever see each other again. They remember boiling soup from the grass in front of the refugee camp. They remember the pain of war. And they hate it. But they also remember their homeland . . . and they love it. I have never experienced, in all my life, a greater example of loyalty or citizenship then my grandparents. My grandparents were real citizens, both of Latvia and America. They had a love for their country, their government, and their roots. Even today, fifty years after they left, when they talk about Latvia, they cry.

Papu loves his homeland, but he is also a faithful American citizen. He pays his taxes, served in the military, and worked as a civil engineer. I've never heard him bash our government. Maybe it was because he'd felt the sting of a Nazi bullet. I've never heard him argue with the police. Maybe it was because he was reunited with his family as U.S. soldiers looked on. I've seen him salute the flag, protect his family, and build his own house. He loves his friends and was loved by his family. I don't remember him ever talking to me about patriotism or citizenship. He simply lived it. And that's what mattered to me.

Here again, we are faced with providing our kids with a value that is unpopular by today's standards. But something of the holy regard for citizenship found in John's grandparents must be passed on to our children. If they have a passion to protect their citizenship, they will live accordingly, knowing that it matters that they are free. As parents, we should model this passion, if not in direct service to our country, then in language that sings of our gratefulness for citizenship.

As citizens of the United States, we live in what most consider the most successful constitutional republic in the world. Our economy is strong, we have great opportunity for average people to excel, and we are producing more than ever before. Now, in the midst of declining crime rates, skyrocketing profits, and the largest construction boom in history, we are faced with the challenge of instilling strong moral fiber and integrity in the next generation. In this great society of freethinking people, we have the privilege and opportunity of influencing those who will determine how our grandchildren will use the wealth that they will inherit. Modeling the way our children should live under government is a conscious choice, one that must be carried out whether we are discussing a *Newsweek* cover story or reacting to another traffic ticket.

CHAPTER
Nine

School: Homework and After-School Specials

A child educated only at school is an uneducated child.

GEORGE SANTAYANA

Author Frank Stockton tells of a king who had a strange way of dealing with lawbreakers. As the tale goes, the king had a coliseum built especially for his unique way of delivering justice. The was built with two doors at the north end of the main arena. Behind one door, a fierce tiger was placed with the front door of its cage open. Behind the other door, the most beautiful and eligible maiden in the kingdom waited. On the day a convict was to be sentenced, he would be brought in to choose his own fate in front of an anxious crowd. The lady and the tiger were placed randomly behind the doors so no one was certain if the prisoner would encounter immediate death or marital bliss. Somehow, the king saw this arbitrary method of sentencing as a sort of ironic justice.

So it happened that the daughter of the king fell in love with a commoner. For months the two had a secret love affair, but one day the young man was seen with the princess, and the unlawful relationship was reported to the king. Furious, the king had the young man captured and declared that the infamous lover would be made to appear in the coliseum. For several weeks, the princess struggled through two horrible recurring nightmares: one in which her lover was married to another, and one in which he was devoured by a tiger.

Before the day of the trial, the princess discovered which doors would hold the tiger and lady, respectively. Having acquired the priceless information, she sent word to her lover that she would give him a signal for which door to choose.

The next day, as the crowd gathered for the event, the young man was escorted out into the arena. The well-built, handsome lover walked slowly to the center of the coliseum. As the crowd fell silent, he glanced quickly at the princess, who carefully raised her right arm and pointed. All eyes were on the young man—no one noticed the gesturing princess. With confidence, the young man walked toward the door on the right and opened it.

What came out . . . the lady or the tiger?

Obviously, the tiger meant that the young man would never marry and the princess would have the satisfaction that her lover could never be untrue. But would that really be the best for her beloved? Of course not! So what did the princess choose—her lover's life at the expense of her love or the loss of her lover to another? The lady or the tiger? The princess had a choice to make. So do we.

As parents, we consistently make judgment calls about our children's futures. Sometimes our choices hurt our children initially, and sometimes our choices hurt us. We've all seen parents make decisions that they felt were right for their child, but the eventual outcome was so negative that they feel as though they let their child die. On other occasions, we've all seen parents make a decision that they know will be best for the future, but in the meantime they risk losing the love of their child.

On the subject of schooling, parents often face "lady or tiger" decisions. In school, children confront a range of important issues: peer groups, extracurricular activities, scholastic achievement, authority, discipline, and motivation. As we sit in the stands and watch our children deal with these issues, it is imperative that we make the best possible choices about their educational experience—choices that bring life to our children while at the same time allowing us to maintain healthy relationships with them.

FINDING AN EDUCATIONAL SYSTEM THAT WORKS

Parents today are faced with more educational options for their children than ever before. Should we stick with the public schools? What about charter schools? Do faith-based schools offer quality education? Complicating matters is the array of conflicting messages coming from academic institutions and culture in general. Teachers' unions are consistently communicating a message that sounds like the latest party line. In contrast to their voices is the constant "I told you so" whisper from private schools, which we could all ignore except for the fact that many of the most outspoken advocates of public education have their children enrolled in private schools. Add to this cacophony the home school advocates who are trumpeting a loud and growing call to home-based education, and you are left with conflicting information, making it impossible to reach a confident decision.

Reading the research results on schooling methods is confusing as well, because research seems to support the arguments of whoever funded or promoted the research. Even the simple question, "When should a child begin formal education?" is answered by special interest groups instead of sustained, balanced research. We haven't had time for enough students to go through a variety of experiences to find out how schooling effects them as adults, so even the best research remains questionable.

We as parents have a dilemma. How can we assure a quality education for our children while at the same time assuring healthy peer involvement and protection? Do we raise our kids according to information that is being fed to us by current in-vogue socio-political groups? Do we experiment on new schooling methods with our children? Obviously, all of us believe in testing ideas and discovering new ways of doing things, but do we have to experiment with *our* children? Do we want our children to be guinea pigs? Do we want them ruined because we tried and failed with something questionable?

As pastors who counsel thousands of families, we have the opportunity to observe a multitude of ways of educating children. Over the years, we have discovered that the best methods are those that incorporate the strengths of all the schooling options. Sometimes it is impossible for families to do anything other than send their children to public schools, which is fine with the right amount of parental involvement, but we have found that the method outlined below works with tremendous success.

As you read this, bear in mind that all of us have many successful schooling options—the one we prefer is not necessarily the best for every family. Each situation must be treated with open-mindedness and, most importantly, a high degree of parental involvement. No matter what schooling method you choose, maintaining a close relationship with your kids and their schools is imperative.

LOVE ME NOW: NEWBORN THROUGH AGE FIVE

If at all possible, a parent or a trusted relative should stay at home with the child from birth through age five. Because mothers understand nurturing so well, it is best if the mother is available to stay home. Most mothers are great mothers and most children bond powerfully with their mother through these years. A peaceful home, walks in the park, visits to the zoo, and preparing the home for the rest of the family can be a special treasure in the first five years of a child's life. In our view, these early years are the most critical to the social, emotional, spiritual, and mental development of a child. Reading books together, visiting friends together, and simply being together is healthy for both the child and mom.

Sounds old fashioned, doesn't it? Maybe grandmother knew something when she said that cuddling is better than day care, microwave dinners in front of the TV, and rushed mornings.

Question: There is no way I can do this. I have to work to meet the needs of our family. I would love to stay home with my newborn, but I don't have a choice. What do you suggest?

If you have to use day care, we highly suggest some type of faith-based licensed day care, consistent with the values, moral standards, and if possible, the faith position of your family. If a local church or synagogue offers licensed day care, consider using them. But make sure you get to know the workers by name and are involved in your child's life and care. Don't let your child just be one more care recipient in some sterile corporate care setting. Children know if they are cared for in a personal way or if they are just one of a group that is being processed.

In his book *Real Boys,* however, Dr. William Pollack, assistant clinical professor of psychiatry at the Harvard Medical School, argues strongly against separating children from their parents too soon. His argument is that many families force their children to disconnect too soon as children going to school and then again when they enter early adolescence by pressing them to prematurely individuate from their families, which causes them to unwisely connect with another group. Our culture is frequently encouraging this disconnection, and we are paying a price for it. We force the disconnection, then wonder why we can't communicate with our kids.

Children can develop naturally and safely in an environment that is in context with their home. We as parents don't give them their best opportunities if we place our children in situations that are too distinct from the culture of our homes. Well-run child care centers are fine for kids if there is a context in the center that connects the child with home. But a sterile academic environment that doesn't connect with the culture or values of home is confusing to our young children and doesn't benefit them. We don't want to warehouse our children; we want to raise them. Our recommendation: marry before children come along, stay married so at least one parent can stay with the children until half-day kindergarten or full-day first grade. ABCs, phonics, and other educational games at home with a parent or relative are better than premature disconnection and the unnecessary subsequent emotional trauma.

BUILDING THE BASICS: ELEMENTARY SCHOOL

Most children are ready for preschool or kindergarten at age five or six, but they are still very vulnerable and innocent. More and more educators are saying that children do better in schools that maintain a cultural and spiritual context with the family. Faith-based schools, for example, offer security, safety, emotional and spiritual consistency, and usually exceptional teaching. So when possible, we encourage families to place their children in elementary school programs that reflect and reinforce the culture of their homes.

Within a few miles of our home are a Presbyterian school, a Lutheran school, a broad-based school sponsored by a group of evangelical Christians, a Catholic school, and an independent charismatic school. In all of these schools, the elementary school curriculum includes faith-based ideals such as the Ten Commandments, the Golden Rule, caring for the poor, and defending social justice. Early education from a healthy faith perspective molds the hearts of children, teaching them how to care for themselves and others. It defines wholesome standards and establishes meaning for their lives.

A good faith-based elementary education is invaluable, especially if your child can be taught from the Bible in a wholesome, positive atmosphere. None of these schools are harsh or dark, and all of them enjoy academic excellence, which has resulted in students' receiving extremely high scores on standardized tests.

Question: This is not 1950. We can't afford this kind of education. I've got to have my children in the local public school. How can I get the best in this situation?

If faith-based education is impossible for you, many school districts are developing charter schools. These are less convenient than the average elementary school because they don't normally provide transportation, and they require parental involvement. These schools are excellent alternatives, but they aren't available everywhere.

Many public schools are excellent, but all of them can become excellent with increased parental involvement. If your child is in the local elementary school, you should be too. We recommend that parents volunteer one day a week in the public school their child is attending. You don't even have to be in the same physical location as your student. You just need to be there, serving the school, helping in the library, reading to kids. If you can develop a relationship with your child's teacher, offer to serve them however they would like. If that is not helpful to them, make yourself available some other way. Don't crusade, just help. Don't be assuming, be a servant. Help, don't hinder. Most public school teachers are overworked and underpaid, and they will appreciate help from parents who are understanding and supportive. And most importantly, your child will feel the difference in your active involvement.

THE WONDER YEARS: JUNIOR HIGH

The middle school years, which in most school districts are grades six to eight, but in some are just grades seven and eight, are years of radical transition. During these years, children's lives begin to take on their own direction. For most, these years are some of the most perilous and confusing in a kid's life. The psychologist Erik Erickson suggested that during adolescence our children must choose between forming a coherent identity or falling prey to a sense of despair and confusion. Issues about sexuality, popularity, dress, and bonding with peer groups become major issues in the mind of the middle school student.

For this reason, we encourage parents, when they are able, to home school during these two or three pivotal years. Many churches now offer home school support systems. Excellent video programs and home curriculum programs are available which allow parents and students to bond in a significant way during these formative years. You will love it; your child will love it. You can make it interesting by traveling, visiting museums, going to historical sites, doing experiments together, growing things together, and learning together. These years can be the backdrop for some of your fondest memories.

Question: Home schooling? Time is worth more than gold in my home right now. I've got other children, a spouse, a home to maintain, and I need to work, at least part-time, just to keep up. I need a better idea for my family.

If home schooling is out of the question, then it's the time to be involved in a great church that is large enough to have a specialized junior high program, or the type of church where your junior high student can build strong social ties. These years cannot be taken for granted, and it's worth making major adjustments to see your child associating with the right people and forming the right attitudes. If your children have to be in public school, be involved in the school and make church a top priority for your children to connect.

THE DISCOVERY YEARS: HIGH SCHOOL

At the end of the eighth- or ninth-grade year, whichever is the beginning of high school for your school district, have a talk with your teen and find out how they want to finish out their basic education. Most will opt for their public high school, which we think is great. They might choose a faith-based school, which is fine if they choose to go there. Faith-based schools are generally not positive experiences for high school students if their parents force them to go. But they are great if the student chooses them. We think the best option for everyone involved, however, is the local public high school.

Why? Because in public high school kids will be exposed to everything the world has to offer and still come home every night. These are the years when the lessons learned while staying home with them in the early years, sending them to a faith-based elementary school, and home schooling them through the junior high years are refined. This is where we teach our children to have personal character, deal with authority, evaluate conflicting ideas, and find their own strength. As crazy as it sounds, these are the years when we actually want them exposed to certain negative opportunities, understanding that they have to come home and talk about it.

In the high school years, the dinner or breakfast table become extremely important, because we want every opportunity to refine and integrate a lifetime of values and training. Coaches, teachers, sexual opportunity, drugs, rebellion, hatred, social reform, tests, parties, and values all crash together in high school. This is when it should happen—the formation of character.

We want them to happen during high school, before college. At college, they don't come home every night. But during high school, we can stay in constant touch. If you miss their high school years, then whatever influence happens to capture their attention during these years will form them. But if you stay involved, which they want you to do, you will teach them to be great people in a mediocre world. They will be creative when others are passive. They will think when others just absorb. They will lead while others only follow. They will be great, because you made a great investment. You are actually raising your children instead of just letting them grow up like a plant or a puppy. You've actually allowed them to become great people.

Question: I don't want to do this! They are too young and vulnerable. I want them in a more protected environment than this. Can't I home school them during their high school years as well?

Yes, you can, but only if they ask for it. We're not saying you should abandon your leadership and let them make all the decisions, but as your teens become more thoughtful, you will make a mistake if you dictate all the major decisions to them. There are a variety of reasons why a child might want to stay at home or in a private school setting, and each of those have to be evaluated as they arise. But generally, children are ready for high school if you'll stay in touch with them. Don't disappear, don't detach, don't think you've finished.

If we do a good job of giving direction and coaching during high school, and insuring that our kids are connected with a strong youth program through our churches, then we'll be pleased with their decisions when they leave for college or the workplace. Once they are gone, they won't have Mom or Dad to influence so many of their decisions, so the high school years are the perfect opportunity to help them integrate their early training and the confusing messages they'll receive from the world at large.

THE RIGHT AMOUNT OF INTERACTION

Peter had walked this way a thousand times before. But today something seemed different. Something was wrong. As he passed the Texaco station, he clenched his book bag and adjusted his jacket. What was wrong with him? It's not like he had any reason to worry. It had been a good day at school, and at fifteen Peter was confident that he could take care of himself. As he rounded the corner onto Oak Street, his heart stopped. Four guys from his school surrounded him. It happened too fast for him to react. It was a flurry of flannel, fists, and faces. That's all he could remember—the faces. For no apparent reason, the four guys from the wrestling team punched, kicked, and tore at him for what seemed like an eternity. It stopped as suddenly as it had started, and they were gone.

When it was over, Peter found himself bawling uncontrollably. Quickly, he got up and ran the rest of the way home. After explaining his bruises and torn shirt to his mom and dad, Peter locked himself in his room, listened to music for a while and went to sleep a different person. That night, life was somehow more real than it had been that morning. As he fell asleep, his mind whirred with a thousand questions. Why did they do it? How should he react? What would tomorrow bring? Meanwhile, another conversation was going on in the living room. Peter's parents had some tough decisions to make. Should they switch schools? Should they tell the school? Should they try to get those boys expelled? Should they even get involved at all?

Peter's story might be a bit extreme, but the reality is that all parents will face situations when they will have to evaluate how to interact with their kids' school. How involved should we be? Where do we draw the line? Good questions. School is that fantastic place full of triumph and failure. It's during the junior high and high school years that teens will experience some of the greatest joys and worst heartbreaks of their young lives, and we must figure out how to coach them through those experiences. The good news is that coaching our kids on how to endure the tough times while enjoying the good times is one of the greatest challenges of being a parent. But because coaching is uncomfortable, because it means getting truly involved with a teenager's life, many parents grow distant from their teens during these years. Never let this happen. Fight the urge to just "let them go." As our teens meander through the tough maze that is junior high and high school, we must learn to guide them through their journey.

In cases such as Peter's fight, the temptation of the parent is to react and defend their son. Certainly, the decision is up to the parents and will vary from scenario to scenario, but the decision to get too involved may not always be the right one. As our teenagers begin to interact with institutions outside the home, part of our role is to coach them on how to deal with problems within those institutions. At times, we must give them good advice and then let them make their own decisions, as painful as that may be. It's important for us to resist the temptation to try to solve our kids' problems for them, even though it's our instinctive nature to do so.

The school system has been set up as sort of a university of life for kids. It operates much like our broader communities, though the consequences are not as severe. For instance, if we cheat on our taxes, we can expect to pay the penalty in finances and possibly time in prison. In high school, if our kids cheat on an exam, they can expect to pay the price of a failed course or possibly time in detention. Our kids learn that their actions have consequences before the consequences really hurt them. As life progresses, the consequences get more and more severe, but hopefully our kids have learned the lesson while still at home or in school. Coaching our kids through bad decisions and the consequences of those bad decisions is part of our responsibility as parents. Embrace the process and avoid the temptation to fight the system in trying to "protect" your child. Of course, always use your own discernment and wisdom in dealing with your teens' school.

COACHING THROUGH FAILURE

Perhaps the preeminent responsibility of parents of teens is to teach them to handle failure. The right response to our kids' failures will mean strengthened character, while the wrong response may deal a devastating blow to their self-esteem and motivation. Acknowledging the importance of coaching through failure is as easy as recalling our own failures as teenagers and all the disappointment associated with those failures. John's foray into high school athletics has always served him as a reminder of the importance of parental guidance in times of failure:

It was the first practice of the year. I had dreamed of playing football ever since I could remember. But I was always too small. At the beginning of ninth grade, I was still small, but I was determined to learn and at least try. I was surprised that Coach Woodard actually let me on the team (although now I understand why: we were a small Christian high school and anybody willing to fill a hole and take a hit was welcomed). I remember the incredible fear I felt as I walked out onto that practice field. I was smaller than most of the guys, and a lot weaker. It was all I could do to stay on my feet most of the practice. I remember how badly I wanted the practice to be over so I could stop. I didn't know anything. I didn't know how to throw a football. I didn't know how to block a defender. I didn't even know what a play was. I was so embarrassed. All I wanted to do was go home. I was a failure and I knew it. I wasn't cut out for football. When the practice got over that afternoon, I was thrilled to see my dad waiting for me in the car, but I was nervous to tell him how I felt. I walked down to the familiar Honda Accord and put my helmet into the trunk. As I sat down on the makeshift plastic seat cover in the passenger seat, I closed the door and stared straight ahead. I didn't even want to look at my dad for fear that he'd watched part of the practice. I had wanted to make him proud of me … and I had failed. Miserably. As we pulled away from the practice field, I decided to quit football. I decided to quit, that is, until my dad said those magic words. He never looked at me. He simply said, "I'm proud of you, John." That was it. That was enough.

Rest assured, in junior high and high school, failure is inevitable. Treasure the times your teens fall down, and help them up and teach them to learn from their mistakes. Some of the greatest moments between parents and teens can happen in the midst of heartbreaking failure. A failed exam. A missed basket. A dropped date. Use failure to your parenting advantage. Remember that failure is only failure if you don't get up again. Part of our responsibility as parents is to help our kids get up.

Eaglets learn their coping skills and develop their ability to fly the same way teens do. When a young eaglet approaches the age of maturity, its mother snatches it up by its feathers, soars into the sky hundreds of feet off the ground and drops the small bird out of its beak. The eaglet will attempt to fly, but if it isn't successful, the mother bird will swoop down under the young bird and rescue it from certain death just in the nick of time. The mother bird knows when it is time for the young bird to learn to fly, but it also is ready to catch it if it falls. We have the same opportunity as our kids reach their teenage years. School is a series of failed flying attempts and rescues, but we must continue to help our teens gracefully and always be willing to drop them, or save them, once again.

As you encourage your child (and yourself) through the schooling process, remember that it truly is possible to raise great kids. As tough as it sometimes seems, having fantastic, successful children is within your reach. Millions of families in a variety of cultures and a variety of economic backgrounds have raised great kids. We already know how to do this. Don't listen to mixed media messages and people who have given up hope. We know we can raise great kids if we will simply decide to do it.

CHAPTER
Ten

Church: How Does Faith Fit In?

The things which are impossible with men are possible with God.

JESUS CHRIST

Steve. He had been in and out of the party scene for years. He was one of the key Extacy (a party drug) dealers for the Boulder and Denver rave scene. For five years, his life consisted of partying, sex, and drugs. He never finished high school, was almost arrested more times than he can remember, and often wondered if life was worth living. And all before the age of twenty-one.

At the end of his rope, he came to . . .

Sally. She was a straight-A student with great parents and a bright future. She excelled at everything she tried but was haunted with a hatred of her physical appearance. During her sophomore year, she embarked on the horrible journey into bulimia. Her mom and dad desperately wanted to help her, but weren't sure what to do.

Then, one Wednesday night, she came to . . .

Jacob. He was the captain of his high school baseball team. By the end of his junior year, he had been offered several college scholarships and even had a few pro scouts looking at him. Jacob was on top of the world. His life was perfect—until his parents filed for divorce. Crushed, Jacob quickly began the downward spiral. He quit the baseball team and turned inward, unlike himself, and plunged further and further into darkness.

Somewhere in the middle of his nightmare, he came to . . .

Rachel. She was the captain of her cheerleading squad, a member of student council, and had just been elected homecoming queen. For her, high school was the time of her life. Rachel was destined to have a great life, and she knew it.

She also knew that she needed help to make good decisions along the way, so she came to. . .

Steve, Sally, Jacob, and Rachel. And they all came to . . . church. Wait. Don't close the book or flip forward to the next section. The ideas here will be incredible tools to help you navigate your teens successfully through their junior high and high school years. The thing the four students above have in common is that they all had guts enough to come to church. That's right, church. "But, isn't church only for old-timers and weak people?" you ask. No, it's not. In fact, the need to develop faith in God is at the core of us all. Read on.

It's funny how we gravitate toward issues of faith during the tough times of our lives. During the Columbine High School tragedy, every high school in Colorado was transformed into a praying school. For a few short moments, the line between church and state was blurred, not only by the words of President Clinton urging a nation to pray but also by the hearts of people looking for answers. The power of faith and prayer was evident in the picture on the front page of the *Denver Rocky Mountain News* featuring a huge circle of teenagers with arms lifted, passionately seeking God for answers and relief. Even now, a month after the tragedy, the signs and banners posted around Denver bare witness to the pull of faith. "Columbine, we're praying for you." "God bless you, Columbine."

Why is this? Deep down, we know that spiritual life makes us complete. We know that life isn't only about jobs, cars, bills, or even families. There is something else. A higher reason. A purpose for being alive. We, the authors, believe that this purpose is found in Jesus, who provided for us a way to live in God. In his teachings, lifestyle, and death, Jesus modeled for us both the reason for our existence and what our response to that existence should be.

Whether or not you believe in Jesus, he made an undeniable impact on the world that must be noted. In his recent book, *The Divine Conspiracy,* Dallas Willard writes,

> Today, from countless paintings, statues, and buildings, from literature and history, from personality and institution, from profanity, popular song, and entertainment media, from confession and controversy, from legend and ritual— Jesus stands quietly at the center of the contemporary world, as he himself predicted. He so graced the ugly instrument on which he died that the cross has become the most widely exhibited and recognized symbol on earth.[5]

We mentioned earlier that parenting requires us to settle the issues of life, and faith is the most significant of those issues. So often, we ignore or disregard the spiritual development of our kids because we're not sure what to say, or we want them to decide for themselves, or we're simply not sure of it ourselves. But without question, the consistent development of the spiritual lives of our teens is vital. Faith radically changed the lives of Steve, Sally, Jacob, Rachel, and literally millions of other teenagers.

A healthy community of faith fosters great teenagers. In the following pages, we'll address some of the critical questions about faith and parenting.

WHAT CAN CHURCH DO FOR MY TEEN?

A good church will help you in your mission to raise kids in five major ways:

- by reinforcing the life skills you've already taught your teen at home
- by offering mentoring to support your role as a parent
- by promoting good decisions in your teen through positive peer influence
- by building confidence and purpose
- by expanding your teen's worldview

Life Skills Reinforcement

A strong community of faith will not only train young people in spiritual matters but will also coach teens in how to live their practical lives. The Bible teaches principles that address all the major issues in life, and any good church will address those same issues. Church groups create opportunities for teens to discuss peer pressure, romantic relationships, work responsibilities, and family concerns, all with life-giving biblical standards. As you participate in a good church with your family, it's important to remember that the church's role is to reinforce what you are already doing as a parent, not actually be the parent. In the difficult task of raising kids, it's easy to look to everyone except ourselves to take care of them. The church can never replace what you do as a parent, but it can be an effective tool in reinforcing what you've already been teaching them.

Susan, the daughter of a friend of ours, was having a rough day at school and decided to walk home. Helen, a friend of Susan's mom at church, saw Susan walking and picked her up, took her home, and on the drive had a tearful heart-to-heart girl talk. Helen was able to reinforce good thinking in a tender moment with Susan, which would not have happened without involvement in a local church.

Successful Mentoring

On the "mountain of life" we all need two kinds of people in our lives: people above us, helping us climb up, and people below us, who we're helping to climb. Without those above us, that is, without parents, teachers, coaches, and pastors, we have a hard time navigating our way successfully. Without people below us, relying on us for assistance, we have little motivation to keep climbing. The key is to have more people above us on the mountain of life than below us. As the laws of physics go, wherever there's more energy being exerted on us, that's where we'll end up. Thus the importance of a good church. A good church will provide the added strength teens need to continue an upward ascent on the mountain of life.

It really does take a community to successfully raise great kids. Part of raising kids is finding people to help you coach them. A good church will offer exactly that. In a good church, your teen will see the heroes and the hurting, the young and the old, the confident and the cowardly, all working together toward the same end—a faithful life. In this world of instant gratification and self-promotion, church offers the age-old principles of giving, helping, and learning that will bring true character into teens' lives.

Positive Peer Influence

"You can't judge my friends!" If you've ever heard these words, you're officially the parent of a teenager. As our kids wander through the maze of their teenage years, they automatically pick up a group of people that will help shape who they will become. After a million after-school specials and motivational school assemblies, we all know the power of peer influence is very real. Our teens' set of friends will be one of the most critical influences on their success. "But how can I pick my teen's friends?" you ask. It's true, you can't exactly force your teen to make friends, but you can help put your teen in an environment where positive peer influence will be the standard. Good churches and many social clubs are great places to set your kids up for positive peer influence.

In any social setting, your teen has the opportunity to either live as a thermometer or a thermostat. A thermometer adjusts to the temperature of the room, but a thermostat actually changes the temperature of the room. In parenting, we want our kids to be the kind of leaders who set the standard for everyone else "in the room." Of course, we all act as thermometers some of the time. That's okay. It's part of life. The key is to ensure that during the thermometer years, when your teen is modeling those around him, he or she has positive people to emulate. In a strong church, your teen will have the advantage of being surrounded by peers who will help him or her make the right positive adjustments in life and character until your teen becomes the one who "sets the temperature."

Always encourage your teen to spend time with people who are "better" in specific areas of life then they are. Playing basketball with people who are more skilled than you will make you a better player. Being in a band with people who are more talented than you will make you a better musician. Studying with someone who is smarter than you will make you a better student. In life, surrounding yourself with people who are "better" than you will make you a better, more complete person. As your teens grow up, help them make acquaintances and friends who are living good lives. Keep in mind that as the parent, you might spot certain friends who will be better influences than others. Remember, you're the parent; it's okay for you to help your teen make the right choices.

Confidence Through Faith

Insecurity is one of the plagues of being a teenager. Maybe it's the awkward and ruthless onslaught of puberty, or maybe it's the constant images of "perfection" jarring at our kids from every media, but the lack of self-esteem is a real and powerful enemy. A lack of self-confidence in a teenager can leave them crippled for days, months, or years. Low self-esteem eats away at the core of a teenager and can turn the most outgoing, happy kid into a depressed, lonely, inward person. Experience has shown us that low self-confidence will eventually affect almost every area of our lives. If it's not handled correctly in junior high and high school it will rear its ugly head later in life. Finding a job will be harder, keeping off excess weight will be more challenging, and maintaining a relationship will be nearly impossible. Without question, one of the most important assignments we have as parents is to rip apart the effects of low self-esteem in our kids so they can journey through life confidently. At church, your teen will find the keys to strong inner confidence.

Faith gives us confidence in life because it reinforces the ideas of individual destiny and purpose. It offers teenagers a purpose bigger than themselves, yanking them out of their comfort zones and into other peoples' lives. It fosters relationships with people whose sole interest is encouraging young people and helping them to succeed. A good church will encourage your teenager in life, build confidence in them, and ultimately help you as a parent in building a strong, confident adult.

WORLDVIEW EXPANDED

Churches offer opportunities for teens to travel to needy areas of the world, from Indian Reservations to distant countries to the inner city of your hometown. Regardless of the destination, these trips invite teens to look beyond themselves and change their perspective on the meaning of life. John's trips with teenagers have given him a reservoir of stories of changed lives:

> Our entire team crowded into the little Chinese flat. We were riveted. . .our hearts were pounding, our minds were whirring, our bodies were frozen. We motioned to the team to sit still. Chinese guards passed by slowly as we crouched in hushed silence. An hour passed and we slowly crept into another room. As our eyes adjusted to the light, we realized why we were there. In solemn silence, we watched as a small group of worshipers gathered to exercise what we sometimes take for granted: the freedom to pray. Our small group of adventurers had traveled thousands of miles to witness this. We were there to pray, to encourage, and most importantly, to learn. And we did. In the darkness of the night, everything we'd been taught about freedom suddenly came alive. For three weeks, we visited small churches, helped to provide

humanitarian aid, and toured the country. The handful of teenagers experienced life as they never had before. By the time their plane touched down back in the USA, a major paradigm shift had taken place in them. They were changed. They thought differently, they acted differently, they spoke differently.

Every summer, our church sends hundreds of teenagers all over the world to experience life in another culture. Visiting everywhere from Kathmandu to Tanzania, they always come home different. The experiences almost always help to create a new sense of gratitude, understanding, and perspective. A broader worldview is established that follows teens through the rest of their lives. Experiences like these and other community, service, and outreach events will help to expand and develop strong personal and spiritual convictions in your kids.

How Do I Choose a Good Church for My Family?

This question inevitably comes up in discussions like these, and for good reason. But finding a good church is a lot easier than you might think. Here are a few simple criteria that you can use in looking for a church for your family:

1. Find a Church That Actually Believes Something

Many churches don't influence their parishioners positively because they don't ascribe to any foundational beliefs. In locating a church, find out what they believe about the Bible and Jesus Christ. If they believe the Bible and believe that Jesus Christ is the Son of God, Savior of the world, then you'll want to keep this church on your list of possibilities.

2. Find a Church That Has a Trustworthy Leadership Team

Several years ago the hit movie *Leap of Faith* featured comedian Steve Martin as a traveling evangelist who used fake miracles and stage tricks to deceive people into giving money to his ministry. Sound familiar? Teenagers have an amazing ability to decipher between a genuine leader and a charlatan, and they'll want to be in a church whose leaders are trustworthy. How can you tell? By finding out how long they have been in the community, their staff turnover, and their accountability structure. Is the Senior Pastor able to be dismissed? If we were looking for a new church, we would want the Senior Pastor to have been in the church for at least four years with a core team that is faithful to him.

3. Find a Church That Already Has a Lot of Kids Around

An important ingredient for our teens is the ability to connect with other teens who have core spiritual values, so a church with a conviction about the importance of young people is vital. If other kids are around, it usually means your kids can meet kids in their own age group and receive positive coaching from others. We're not saying that church kids are perfect, but we are saying that we want our kids to have friends who have values and beliefs consistent with our own.

4. Find a Church That Is Respectful Toward Other Churches in the Community

While driving in Florida last year, we noticed a billboard for a local church that read, "Come to _____ Church—it's the friendliest church in town!" The pastor of that church is inadvertently saying, "Every other church in town isn't really that friendly." As you select a church, find one whose pastor models for your teens how to treat other churches in your city. Because of the importance of high school Christian clubs that have students in them from various churches, we don't want our family to connect with a church that has a hostile, arrogant, or exclusive posture against other churches. Ask the church leadership about their relationship with several other key churches in the community. Their response will communicate whether or not they are connected with the other churches or if they have become excessively independent.

5. Find a Church with Engaging Worship and Impacting Teaching

Several weeks ago, we celebrated the Fourth of July here at New Life Church. The service opened with a trip back in time as a man dressed in buckskin warned the congregation that "the British are coming!" Ted interrupted the centennial character to orient the crowd, and then the drama continued. We then embarked into a worship service that included both contemporary praise and contemplative hymns. The sermon that morning was both patriotic and biblical—an exhortation on the theology of America. We received more positive mail about that morning's service than any other in the past six months. We were reminded that people are hungry for genuine worship and impacting teaching. Your teen will not tolerate a politically correct church that is simply into social positioning. They want their church to offer core foundations for living with a dynamic spiritual strength. Creative, innovative churches are becoming the strongest churches in the world, and your teen will love being a part of those churches.

6. Find a Church That Has a Global Vision

For your teenager to be a great kid, he or she needs to be involved in a church that has dynamic church camps, short-term missions trips, and cross-cultural training. We don't expect any church to offer all of these things all of the time, but the church you choose for your family should have a global perspective, a vision that goes beyond the church walls. Here at New Life, flags from every nation in the world fly from the ceiling of our sanctuary, and the walls of our youth chapel are covered with a mural of the world. The purpose of the church should never be the church. Instead, the purpose of the church should be those outside its walls. When your teen is exposed to this type of spiritual insight, they will become great people.

7. Find a Church That Is Spirit-Filled

This simply means that you should choose a church that has a spirit of grateful worship. Churches are not clubs, social organizations, or reform schools: they are believers' meetings. Find a church that does not hesitate to encourage your teenager to be dominated by God's Spirit. Churches should encourage our teens to be filled with God's Spirit of love, joy, peace, patience, kindness, goodness, faithfulness, gentleness, and self-control (Galatians 5:22–23). The church you choose should encourage the gifts of the spirit (1 Corinthians 12–14), adherence to the Ten Commandments (Exodus 20:1–17), and the discipline of daily prayer and Bible study. These disciplines in a spirit-filled environment will give your child every opportunity to develop the attributes of a wholesome lifestyle.

How Do I Get My Family Involved in Church?

Once a church is chosen, the family has to connect. We believe that churches are, in essence, an extended family. When you choose a church, the first few times you visit, you are guests. You shouldn't expect to instantly connect with people—just begin the process of getting comfortable. Once the final decision is made to make a particular church our church home, you are asking to be adopted by the church family.

If you have young children in your family, begin by volunteering in the children's department. And don't just serve for a short time: go as a husband-wife team if possible and volunteer to serve your child's Sunday School teacher for at least a year. After that, serve as an usher, a greeter, a janitor on Saturday mornings, or whatever is needed. Make yourself and your family members available. When a family makes the church the central focus of their family, that family takes on a purpose and depth that it wouldn't normally have. But you have to do it as a family, not just Dad at the church all the time with Mom and the kids at home, or Mom at prayer meetings all the time and the kids feeling abandoned.

All churches, from time to time, have internal problems, just like any family. When those problems surface, the same wisdom that we use in our homes with family difficulties has to be used in dealing with church problems. Among this authorship team, Ted has been at New Life Church for fourteen years and John has been there for four years. We have had some wonderful times at New Life, and we have had our share of trying moments as well. But our families connect here, we grow old gracefully together here, and we are stronger together here at the church than we could ever be alone. Good churches are worth connecting to and raising our children in. They help make our families great.

HOW TO RELATE WITH YOUR PASTOR

David came home from church upset at the youth pastor. "I got kicked out of the youth meeting tonight because the guy next to me was making noise. I didn't do anything wrong, and now they won't let me come back. I'm glad. I hate that place anyway, the bunch of hypocrites."

Mom and Dad have a choice to make when this happens. Some will call the church to find out what really went on. Others will join with their child's judgment and agree that the youth pastor shouldn't have done that and let their child stop going to the youth meeting or switch churches, trying to find a place where their child is more happy. Wise parents, though, will coach their child in dealing with their youth pastor.

"David, you know that you have a responsibility to work with your pastor. Give him a call tomorrow and explain what happened to you and see what you can work out. I'm sure he'll be reasonable with you."

The goal is to insure that the youth pastor has the freedom to work with your child, knowing that you will coach the child but not take up any offense or lose confidence in the youth pastor's ability to coach your child.

Several weeks ago we had to deal with a situation where one child offended another child. As the two children squabbled, both sets of parents became involved and, as a result, started to involve not only the youth pastors but the executive pastoral staff as well. At the core of the problem was the fact that the parents would not allow the pastors to pastor their children. They wanted to fight it out with the other parents. They wanted their children's rights protected. They wanted to be sure that justice was done for their children.

As a result, the pastor ended up being a referee between two sets of parents, and both children missed an opportunity to learn how to relate to other kids and grow in personal responsibility. Because the parents didn't know how to relate to the pastor and how to trust the pastor to pastor their kids, the kids missed a life-lesson, or, rather, learned a bad one.

If your child is part of a youth group, let the pastors do their job of mentoring your kid. Trust them. Honor them. Realize that pastors are human, that they will make mistakes, but that their role is invaluable in your teen's ability to learn life's lessons.

So, What Happened to Steve, Sally, Jacob, and Rachel?

Last night John got a call from Steve.

"John, Ashley's pregnant," Steve said excitedly. Last year John had the privilege of standing in front of Steve and Ashley as they gave their lives to each other in selfless sacrifice. Steve has not only become a great husband, but he's become an incredible leader and positive influence on everyone he comes in contact with.

Last week, John sat amid three thousand people as Sally walked across the platform to receive her diploma. Her hollow eyes had been replaced with a look of confidence and hope.

Jacob went on to play for a minor league team right out of high school and has learned to forgive his parents and deal with his pain through Jesus.

Rachel is still actively involved in the church youth group and her school.

These kids' lives were strengthened and changed through faith in God. There's no question that a good church will help your kids grow to become healthy, happy adults.

PART
Four

Confident
Parenting

CHAPTER
Eleven

Boys Into Men

*There comes a time in every rightly constructed boy's
life when he has a raging desire to go somewhere and
dig for hidden treasure.*

MARK TWAIN

DEFINING MOMENTS — BECOMING A MAN

For the American Indians, it is a Vision Quest. For the boys of
Papua New Guinea, it's a weeklong ritual. For the fourteen-year-
old in Alaska, it's his first hunt. For the nervous adolescent in Los
Angeles, it's learning to drive. Somehow, every boy, either by intent
or by instinct, is pushed through its threshold. Every boy must pass
through it. Every boy must endure it. It stands like an ominous
river threatening all that dare to meander at its edges. It's a river
named Adolescence. The sign on the bank says "Rite of Passage."
And along the banks are milestones that stand as evidence of con-
quest. Somewhere along the watery journey, it empties into a magnificent body of water called Manhood.

Who can adequately describe a boy's journey into manhood? Writers have explored the tumultuous adventure for centuries and in a variety of ways. Shakespeare's Romeo left his childhood behind when he discovered love. Charles Dickens' Pip was thrust into maturity by his mysteriously great expectations. Mark Twain's Tom Sawyer stumbled into life's stark reality when he got stuck with a criminal in a cave. To be sure, a boy's journey into manhood is a mysterious process, one that is full of excitement and fear and hope and joy and adventure.

Before we begin to discuss specifics, we'd like to tell you one of the best boy-to-man processes we've ever heard of. For five years during the Cold War, Ted was a youth pastor for a church in Louisiana. The church felt its young men needed to understand the global conflict between capitalism and communism and its implications for believers. Even though the church's cause wasn't political, the high school students who attended the church had to understand the terror that people of faith faced when they lived in an atheistic state. The thought of the government imprisoning parents because they believed the Bible, or pastors being executed for publicly praying, or fellow teens disappearing in the night, never to be heard from again because they mentioned to their younger sibling that they believed in God, was totally foreign. The boys who were consumed with sports, women, and personal appearance needed to be coached into men who could make a significant contribution for the benefit of others—perhaps even for the world. Boys into men. That was the goal.

The way to achieve that goal was found on Agony Island, an uninhabited desert island an hour off the coast of Mississippi. Every summer, Ted's church would take a group of boys to the island for a week to teach them survival, teamwork, trust, and a host of other lessons that can only be learned in unusual circumstances.

The Agony Island trip was jam-packed every year. Boys would look forward to it for years, waiting for their opportunity to go. Agony Island wasn't the island's official name; the boys had named it that in honor of their suffering. Just a little brush grows on the three-quarter-mile-long and quarter-mile-wide stretch of shell and scrub. The warm waters of the Gulf of Mexico that surround the island swarm with every imaginable form of sea life, from friendly dolphins to biting crabs. It could be a vacationer's paradise or a stranded person's hell—all at the same time.

Every year, each boy was allowed to bring a small tent, a pillow, a gallon of water, and an egg. In addition, the whole group would bring along one pig. That's right—one pig. In the adolescent's heaven of a busload of friends, laughter, and great music, the group would always begin to divide into two—those who wanted to name the pig and make him a pet, and those who wanted to kill and eat the pig.

After arriving at the shore and loading on the fishing boat for a one-hour trip to the island, it would dawn on each of the young guys that there wasn't a McDonalds to go to or a Mommy to call. As the day wore on, their faces would begin to show the horrible recognition of what was meant by the term they had heard for the first time a few weeks before: "rite of passage." This trip was going to be tough. It would hurt. To endure it would be something significant. And there was no way out. No radio, no cell phones, no back-out plan. The only end would be the end. Crying, complaining, whining, or fighting wouldn't make any difference. It was like being in hell—there was no turning back.

The boat would always arrive at the island when the mid-afternoon sun was at its hottest point. The crew would unload, pig and all, thoughtfully review with the captain the pick-up date and time, and then, hesitatingly, as a group, wave good-bye to the captain.

As the days would pass, dark clouds of mosquitoes would attack day and night. In the middle of each sweltering day, the group would try to hide from the heat in the water, only to be bitten by sea urchins. Water supplies would begin to run out, and hunger would cause everyone to lose interest in the pig's name. They'd remember that it was only a pig, after all, and that meant bacon and ham. On Agony Island, killing and eating, thinking and surviving, connecting with others for strength, and fighting with others unnecessarily all took on new perspective. There was no way to get away from those you hated. There was no way to relieve the discomfort. Everyone had to stick together, regardless of feelings. They were on an island together, until the end. It was up to the group to decide what the island would make of them.

Actually, no one's life was ever in danger, but the boys never knew that. In their minds, they had to stay together, they had to stay healthy, they had to ration everything in order to be okay when the boat returned. And it always did return—to a group of men who had learned to be their best. They had learned how to care for one another, how to pray, the reason for killing, the reason for loving, and the penalty of selfishness. No one came back from Agony Island a loner, a pervert, or an antisocial hyper-independent rebel. It just didn't happen. Instead, they became interconnected men, having talked about sex, relationships, governments, people, God, and purpose. They knew more about life. They had become substantive people. They knew suffering. They knew manhood. They were ready to begin.

Unfortunately, we can't take all the teenage boys we know out to Agony Island for a week (and after reading that story, you may not want to!). But we still must train boys on becoming men. We must teach them real lessons and encourage them as they encounter real struggles. As boys live through their second decade, they will encounter seven major milestones. Each milestone represents a new level of discovery, and a new chance to enter into a successful manhood.

SEVEN MILESTONES OF MANHOOD

1. Identity—Discovering who he is
2. Interdependence—Discovering how he fits
3. Responsibility—Discovering what he does
4. Sexuality—Discovering self-discipline
5. Money—Discovering stewardship
6. Thought and Opinion—Discovering his mind
7. Position—Discovering his place

1. Identity—Discovering Who He Is

Every boy goes through a series of events that help him define his identity. As he grows, he discovers his interests. Does he like learning? Music? Sports? Reading? Movies? Rockets? Sex? His interests, heroes, and friends begin forming him. His experiences outside the family highly influence him. His life begins taking on its own values. Until now, he was content to live vicariously through his mom and dad, and now for a moment he shares the chisel with his parents as he chips and knocks away at himself in a search for significance. That is the process that we must intentionally guide, or else it becomes a random series of events that sometimes produces good people but often produces people who waste their lives.

As your boys charge through this phase of adolescence, fight the temptation to block or bolster their effort. As parents, our instinct is either to over-protect or over-project our kids as they're figuring out who they are. You are the ones to whom he will look in this process, so allow your own life to be the model for him. But watch out—don't look for a carbon copy of yourself. Don't try to stuff a round peg into a square hole. We've all witnessed the tragedy of children forced into their identity by a parent determined to relive childhood through their teenager. Place the right parameters and influences around your son and then allow him to discover who God made him to be. You'll be delighted at the remarkable result, even if your son's choices are something of a surprise. Ted's father, for instance, never suspected that Ted would want to be a pastor.

My dad attended church, but he had a low regard for pastors. He didn't have confidence in the church, organized religion, or people who were overly outspoken about their faith. He wanted all of his kids to be "Christians," but he didn't want the wars between various streams in the church to infect our hearts. He wanted us to remain innocent.

I'll never forget the expression on his face when I told him that I thought I was supposed to go to school to become a pastor. He looked down, took a long pause, and then responded in a supportive but cautious way. He'd learned the balance of letting me find my own identity, while at the same time cautioning me about potential dangers. Because of his steady direction, his oldest son is a business owner, his second an educator, his third a pharmacist, his fourth a pastor. One of my sisters is a homemaker and the other is a pharmacist. Each discovered their own identity, none were left alone to do it on their own, but none were discouraged to pursue their individual dreams.

The balance of allowing our children their own lives while at the same time ensuring that they are part of the whole family is the tightrope that we all walk. With a healthy identity and an understanding of family, boys will be on the road toward manhood and traveling along toward the next milestone: interdependence.

2. Interdependence–Discovering How He Fits

On the other side of healthy independence is interdependence: lifelong commitments, genuine friendships, family, and faith. Boys are independent, men are interdependent–they've learned where they fit, where they need support, where they can lend support. Homes, churches, schools, neighborhoods, and clubs are all institutionalized interdependence. They encourage us to integrate ourselves into the lives of those around us for a purpose greater than ourselves. Interdependence produces remarkable strength from complementing skills, talents, and experiences in the tapestry of community.

Boys will tend toward interdependence naturally, and we must guide and encourage that tendency. Never make the mistake of thinking boys should be too tough or independently minded, or that they will not long for emotional connection. Such thinking is part of what William Pollack calls the old "Boy Code." Although society has taught us that "boys–and men–are less in need of friends, close personal bonds, or connections," the truth is that close friendships "are of paramount importance to boys."[6]

As your boy grows up, intentionally involve him in family events, decisions, and rituals. Coach him on personally excelling for the good of the group. A great, practical book on this subject is Robert Lewis's *Raising A Modern-Day Knight: A Father's Role in Guiding His Son to Authentic Manhood*. As interdependence is discovered and embraced, responsibility naturally develops and roles become clear. Married men who are independent usually end up divorced or abusive. Married men who understand interdependence are responsible husbands and fathers and are usually highly esteemed and honored by their wives and children. The teaching of interdependence takes place on the football field, the basketball court, at band practice, in a school play, the battlefield, or a campout. When the group wins, everyone wins. When the team loses, everyone loses. That's interdependence.

3. Responsibility—Discovering What He Does

As boys become men, a sense of responsibility replaces boyish freedom. Responsibility is part of the process of growing up, and it's vital to raising great young men. As boys grow up, they'll begin to understand and embrace a sense of who and what they are geared to protect. Where once a boy was happy to nail a sign bearing the words "No girls allowed" proudly on his wobbly wooden fort, now he bears the responsibility to honor, protect, and serve his wife and family. As your son attempts to cross the mark into manhood, help him learn how to handle responsibility by giving him a little, watching him succeed or fail, and then coaching him how to do it better next time. Eventually, you'll witness a boy who has not only become a man but a boy who's become a leader of men.

Responsibility can't be taught through a formula; it must be taught intuitively. Responsibility isn't merely the handling of duties; it is the handling of a life. It is the ability to live for others instead of yourself. Some would say making the bed, cleaning the room, and helping wash the dishes after a meal are where responsibility is taught. That is a portion of what is meant by "responsibility," but that's all. Sometimes these rituals create abusive situations where parents are tyrants and chores are slave labor. Without a doubt, basic responsibilities with consequences and rewards are necessary tools, but our children are not dogs to be trained or horses to be broken; they are kids. They have a spirit, a mind, and a body. They have to learn to care. They have to be people.

We've observed that children raised with handicapped siblings become remarkable people. Likewise, children whose parents are in a public service profession often become outstanding citizens. Children whose parents teach them about helping others by giving to the poor or volunteering at the homeless shelter are likely to be exceptional adults. Why? Because they are responsible. They care. They live for others. Again, Ted learned this lesson well from his father.

> When I was fifteen, two days after Christmas my dad heard me bragging to a boy from a poor family about all the presents I'd received for Christmas. Dad called me into his office, told me that I was to give the boy all of the gifts that I had been bragging about, and that I was to be happy doing it. I went out of his study, went up to the boy and told him that I wanted to give him some of the gifts that had been given to me, and then proceeded to give him all of the gifts that I'd been bragging about. That did it for me. I learned that everything we have is a gift that we can use for ourselves or use for the good of others. That's responsibility. That's becoming a man. I learned that I wasn't just exclusively responsible for my own life but also for the lives of those around me.

4. Sexuality—Discovering Self-Discipline

As boys become men, everything changes, including their bodies and their libidos. The truth is that as boys mature, they quickly become ready to reproduce. As parents and mentors, this incredible stage of life presents for us an opportunity to teach them the value of love and the complexity of managing acceptance and rejection. In the spinning world of adolescent hormones, deciphering the difference between love and instinct can mean the difference between heartbreaking mistakes and a great adult sex life.

We've all heard people talk about the time they had "the big sex talk" with their dad. Some of those talks were beneficial, certainly, but most of them are the source of jokes because they were awkward for both dad and son. Sexuality is too big of an issue to talk about once and then let the chips fall where they may. Here's another approach: let those talks happen naturally, and let them happen frequently. Boys are interested in sex, so don't let it be a taboo subject. Boys naturally talk about sex with their friends when they are in a comfortable situation: a camp out, a retreat, the locker room, the lunch table, or while staying at someone else's house. Some of these conversations might be helpful, but most of them are not. But boys will talk, and it's best for them to know the right thing to say.

Our policy is to answer every question that is asked according to the age that the boy is when he asks it. Then, provide an environment for discussions in wholesome atmospheres. In healthy church youth groups, for example, subjects like masturbation, pornography, homosexuality and bisexuality, and the value of chastity are openly discussed. As things happen at home, in movies, and among friends, you will have plenty of opportunity to talk with your boys about these subjects. Remind them that, no matter what society suggests, love is not random. We can choose who we love, and we had better make good choices. Ted's older kids have heard him go on and on about friends who have gotten in trouble because they became sexually active for the wrong reasons. He also maintains one other policy with his older teens:

> I have a promise with my kids that they can talk to their youth pastor or anyone on the youth staff about anything and I'll never ask the youth staff to tell me about it. I trust them. I respect the fact that in certain stages of life, it's awkward to talk to Mom or Dad about certain issues or interests,

but I want to ensure that someone is in my children's lives that they can talk to who will give them wholesome advice. I don't have the same trust in the school on this issue, but I do trust our church. And I know that as time passes, everything will be discussed at home. I just don't want to force it.

Often sex issues for teens have little to do with love, making it all the more necessary for them to learn the meaning of life. Love is a willingness to live for the other's best interest. It's a commitment. It's an action word. The fact that feelings accompany love is not the primary motivation, because feelings come and go. And if love leads us to a commitment of marriage, then sexual activity within marriage is healthy and wonderful. That's why virginity is a virtue. With this perspective, discussions of pornography, masturbation, homosexuality, and other issues help our families grow in a wholesome direction.

5. Money–Discovering Stewardship

Some say it makes the world go round. Some say it's the root of all evil. Regardless of your view of money, there's no question that it's one of the most powerful tools in shaping the life of your young man. Boys use other people's money, but men earn their own money. Boys need to learn the value of hard-earned compensation for a job well done. So many teenagers today are handed the world by parents who desperately want to connect, but can't find the time. Dollars can be given in lieu of time, but they will always fall short of hours, minutes, and days. Fight the temptation to give your son too many handouts, and encourage him to earn the money he spends. In the process, you'll empower him to value work, money, and time, which will plant in him a greater sense of purpose and perspective in everyday life.

One of the greatest ways to teach your teenager responsibility and stewardship is to help him obtain and manage a checkbook. It's a great idea for teens to learn financial responsibility while still at home as opposed to learning the hard way with creditors calling and bills piling up later in life. Teach your boy how the financial system works and encourage him to begin to be accountable for his own money. Knowing that your teen will be looking to you as a financial mentor will also help you get better control over your own spending and saving habits.

As young people begin to understand the value of hard work and see the wonder of free enterprise at work in our society, many of them will want to try out their own wings in business. As children become teenagers, the lemonade stand in front of the house might turn into a graphic design business or a foray into the world of baby-sitting. Encourage your kids to pursue their business interests while keeping an eye on them to be sure their studies and relationships don't suffer.

Ted's daughter, Christy, expressed an interest in animals when she was a little girl, and when she was thirteen she told her parents she wanted to start a business. Within twelve months, she was earning over $8,000 a year boarding, breeding, and training dogs. Ted's son Marcus was trying to think of a creative way to earn money for an upcoming overseas trip when he got an idea that proved to be a great solution. During the summer of 1997, Colorado experienced a shortage of hay for feeding livestock. Marcus found a farmer in Wyoming with an excess of hay and brought it to Colorado where he sold it at a premium and made just enough to pay for his trip to China. You could easily find dozens of similar stories, and the moral of each story is that teens learn financial responsibility best by actually doing it themselves.

6. Thought and Opinion—Discovering His Mind

As young men begin to accept responsibility, find their place, and earn their way, a sense of value is soon attached to what they think. Responsibility well taken gives way to confidence, which fuels thought and opinion and ultimately gives way to a distinct voice. Encourage your young man to develop the art of critical thinking. Encourage him to read well, assimilate well, and articulate well. Develop avenues for thoughtful discussion between you and your teen. Dinner table debates. After school conversations.

Late night musings about the state of current affairs. If you expect your teen to think well, you have to be willing to do your own due diligence. Read the newspaper. Keep up with the local, national, and global news. Give yourself a primer on issues so you can be the stimulus for your teens' mental journey. John remembers the joy of thinking and talking with his dad:

> My dad had studied philosophy at Stanford University in California and the University of Cape Town in South Africa. He speaks three languages fluently and has taught both Latin and Greek at the university level. Needless to say, Dad is an interesting and versatile conversationalist. Dad loves to read. Over the years, he has amassed a huge collection of books on politics, religion, philosophy, and classic literature. I still remember walking into his library as a child and admiring the volumes that were there. He had books on every subject under the sun. It was there that I first fell in love with books and writing. Of the hundreds of books, there was always one series that stood out to me: the Britannica Great Books. In this collection were the greatest works of the modern world. The works of Plato, Freud, and Marx were together with Dickens, Melville, and Shakespeare. Dad and I devoured the ideas in these books in late night conversations and weekend road trips. I still remember discussions of politics, current affairs, and philosophy over coffee and hot chocolate. These conversations were the foundations to a broad base of thought and opinion that have helped to shape who I am today. Last fall, I received a gift in the mail from my parents ... the Britannica Great Books. Now I can look forward to helping my son, Harrison, develop his own mind.

Help your teen develop his mind and encourage him to begin to think for himself. Begin a practice of finding out what he thinks and how he feels about a subject. Challenge him to defend his position on controversial topics. Teach him to begin to think logically and intentionally. A great exercise in thought is challenging each other in lateral thinking. You can purchase fun and challenging lateral-thinking puzzles and books at your local bookstore or on the Internet. Take the journey into the world of thought and opinion with your teen and challenge him to expand who he is. You'll love the process as you help to create a great mind and get to know your son better in the process.

7. Position—Discovering His Place

On the journey into manhood, somewhere along the path every teenage boy attempts to discover his position. Along with position comes power, authority, and additional responsibility. As parents, we can strategically work to help our kids assume the best positions. In the struggle of manhood, boys will attempt to find position one way or the other, with a good crowd or bad, with the right girl or the wrong one. It's our job to help encourage them as they assume healthy, positive positions in life.

This is tough in our generation because we send confusing messages about men and masculinity. With open debates about the appropriations, or lack thereof, of gender-specific roles, we often emasculate young men or force them to polarize in a macho image that is not helpful. In our church, we offer a great program for young men that encourages a healthy role that is at once masculine and emotionally transparent and sensitive to others. Our young men learn the "manly" stuff like rugged camping, international travel to exotic, difficult locations, and they also explore the protector/provider role of men—but never to the detriment of women. Churches and families can define roles and help young men find their place with healthy balance.

We believe it takes strong men to mold young men into good men. If a woman is a single parent, exposing her sons to healthy role models in the church and community is helpful. If the family is intact, and Dad and Mom have extended family members who are close by, young men thrive. Prisons, adult bookstores, bars, and psychiatric institutions all remind us of the importance of raising boys well—these institutions are full of men searching for answers. Rather than having to answer the confused questions of damaged men, it's better not to damage them in the first place. Instead, raise them in healthy homes with strong support systems. Then we get good young men.

CHAPTER
Twelve

Girls Into Women

*She is clothed with strength and dignity; she can laugh
at days to come.*

PROVERBS: THE ADMIRABLE WOMAN

Ted remembers bringing his firstborn child home from the hospital as if it happened yesterday:

Gayle and I looked like the perfect Norman Rockwell painting. Backs straight, eyes open wide and staring straight ahead, faces pale, and afraid to speak a word, we drove home from the hospital that day with our little bundle, a baby girl. We felt like very different people than the two excited lovers who had arrived at the hospital a few nights before, anticipating the joys, the pain, and the adventure of childbirth.

We were different. We were parents. And this beautiful little curly-headed wonder was our little girl. We knew the question going through both of our minds on that silent drive home was, "What now?"

Daughter. The very word stirs up endless emotional connotations: sensitive, gentle, giggly, pretty, sweet, emotional, tearful, moody, tenderhearted, persuasive, kind. A daughter can bring such sweetness to a home and such turmoil all in the course of an hour. Most parents can read their sons like a book, but who's to know the mind of a daughter? She is a study of a different kind. But what maturity, patience, and love await the parent that pursues it. After all, it is our children who help us grow up. We must accept that a daughter is a special gift to us who is worth getting to know and learning to understand.

THE UNIQUENESS OF RAISING DAUGHTERS

Christy and her dad got up early one morning and went to the barn to saddle the horses. Christy had been riding for years, and her dad had been to some of her shows to see her ride, but they seldom rode together. But this morning was special. Christy had asked her dad to ride to a special field with her and see where she often went to be alone with nature and with her horse. As they rode together along the gravel roads leading to the pasture, they talked about special things. The air was fresh, the sun was rising, and the grass was green. With the Rocky Mountains looming in the background, the setting couldn't have been more perfect.

When they arrived at the field neatly surrounded by forest, they rode from one end to the other, sensing the strength of the horses, the beauty of nature, and the joy of being together. Then Christy asked her dad to stay where he was so she could show him what her horse, Quality Controlled, could do. She trotted to the opposite end of the field and started riding back at full speed. With her hair blowing back, Christy became one with the horse as she raced through the pasture. It scared her dad, invigorated her horse, and made her proud. She was accomplished, and her dad saw her. She had his full attention, admiration, and could feel his concern and desire to protect her. But he couldn't, she was free, yet he still loved her and she felt it. All of these emotions and more ran together in those few brief moments. It was a scene from a multimillion dollar movie. It was the best of life. It bonded Dad and daughter forever.

Raising daughters into young women is a fine art. Little girls are very sensitive to appreciation and affirmation, acceptance and rejection, the tone of saying, "I love you," the kisses and hugs. Little girls are sensitive to many of the subtle things their parents, particularly their fathers, say or do, like their dad glancing at other women at the mall. They love to honor their dads, which means if Dad is dishonorable, it deeply affects the daughter. The same goes for mothers: if either of the parents say something risqué around the house, our daughters won't comment, but they'll remember. We're their model.

The sparkle in a daughter's eye when she sees her dad reveals how little girls see their dads as god-like images and often translate that image, good or bad, to their opinion of God himself. A daughter derives ideas from her father about what men look for in a woman, what pleases a man, what is right or wrong with femininity, and what is acceptable for a woman. They watch and listen as Dad and Mom relate to one another, and that relationship, more than any other influence, establishes their models for male/female roles, family relationships, and prepares them for a life of security or insecurity. When dads cherish the femininity of their daughters, it helps their daughters accept and enjoy being a woman.

Affirming Femininity

Unfortunately, in a society where women are not valued for their womanliness and femininity is misunderstood and often abused, women have had to resort to masculine expression to gain worth and to protect themselves. Several years ago, Ted's wife, Gayle, observed a family scenario she'll never forget. She was leaving a K-Mart when she noticed a father shoving his young daughter out the door. Once they reached the other side, he kicked the little girl in the seat of her pants and yelled at her, his face only inches from hers. The girl's face was white with fear, yet tearless.

Apparently she was accustomed to this type of treatment. Gayle looked around for the mother, who she found standing sheepishly by with her two other children, looking embarrassed and weak.

Perhaps this little girl had behaved badly in the store or had begged for something her father wouldn't or couldn't buy for her. Yet, his response to her no doubt left an indelible impression on her of his low opinion of her and her worth. Gayle made a point to catch eyes with this man, hoping to communicate through her glare how inappropriate his behavior was and to cast a sad reproof for his destruction of the office of father in the eyes of this young girl.

We can easily project what has happened to that girl since that time: she has slipped further and further into insecurity and doubt, loneliness, and fear. We can also project what happened in that marriage. At some point that mother had enough, and the marriage ended in divorce. The daughter probably developed a hatred of men and a hatred for the weakness of women. Her response may have been to develop a more masculine approach to life because she didn't want to be the "weak, abused woman." This often happens to many daughters of divorced parents, especially when the father has left the family, rejecting them by not providing for them or abusing them in any way. These daughters may develop a dislike for men and take on masculine roles and expressions as a means of self-protection. Or sometimes they appear to go the other direction, developing a love-hate relationship with men, dressing in overly provocative clothing and having shallow sexual relationships while looking for masculine love and acceptance.

In either case, what we really have is a broken heart and dashed dreams, expectations, and desires. Little girls need their daddies to be their heroes. They need to know their daddies will protect them and provide for them. In this safety, girls can freely develop their God-given femininity and grow into the fullness of their womanhood.

If a daughter knows her father accepts her, she can enjoy being a girl and can develop into a womanly woman, a lady. This acceptance is enhanced when the mother communicates her own joy in being a woman and teaches the value of womanliness to her daughter.

Our society as a whole has not sent this message to women. Instead, young girls have been made to feel that to lead valuable lives they must compete with men in the workplace. Women should be free to compete in the workplace, but for the last couple of generations we have raised our daughters to believe having a career outside the realm of home and family was the only real way to make a valuable contribution to the world. Now, some leading feminists are beginning to recognize that something is missing from their lives. In her book, *What Our Mothers Didn't Tell Us: Why Happiness Eludes the Modern Woman,* Danielle Critendon says, "We define equality in terms of being the same as men. That has led us to a lot of unhappy destinations. A lot of unhappy lives." In describing the ultra-feminist lifestyle, she goes on to say, "So long as we insist on defining our identities only in terms of our work, so long as we try to blind ourselves to the needs of our children and harden our hearts against them, we will continue to feel torn, dissatisfied, exhausted."

Too little value has been given to the feminine roles of loving and nurturing a family. When girls grow up in confusion about femininity, they lose the innate characteristics for tenderness, caring, and bringing beauty into their world that are uniquely feminine. Certainly not all little girls grow up, marry, and have children. But all have the right to develop and appreciate their femininity and bring it into their adult lives, and even their careers, if that is what they choose. It's okay for girls to be girls.

Thankfully, we in western civilizations have finally accepted the equality of women and men. But it's time we move past the idea that *equal* means *same.* It's time we place value on the idea that womanliness is as wonderful as manliness, and we must teach this to our daughters. It's okay to teach our daughters that their bodies are different than boys' bodies for a reason, and that their bodies serve a purpose that fits in with the whole scheme of femininity. Since the beginning of humanity, women have played an essential role in procreation. In fact, everything about a woman's soft design speaks of nurturing. Whether or not a woman ever has a baby does not diminish the nurturing abilities within her. Early on, girls begin to show tendencies for nurturing those they love through dolls, animals, other children, or babies. This can be seen in women all over the world. This part of a woman's femininity is very beautiful when given full expression. We saw it valued in the lives of Mother Teresa and Princess Diana, who cared for children, the sick, and the needy, and who for many years topped the list of the world's most admired women. We can teach our daughters that the nurturing part of them is admirable and valuable to everyone's lives as well as fulfilling to their own.

In doing this we also teach them the value of their bodies. They have a special gift with the ability of giving life to others (whether physically or emotionally), and that gift must be protected and not given away cheaply. Within the love and safety of marriage, a woman can give the full expression of her body, sharing sexual love with her husband and giving nurture to her children. This is why a young woman should guard against premarital sex and be careful about who she marries.

Another aspect of femininity that should be affirmed in our daughters is a desire or ability to bring beauty into their worlds. This not only includes personal beauty, which comes primarily from the heart, but also their ability to bring beauty to their surroundings. This may not be evident from the appearance of your daughter's bedroom, or, more particularly, her bathroom. But beauty is a work in progress. Order comes eventually. And by appreciating our daughter's particular expression of beauty, whether it be personal, or in clothing, decorating, preparing food, or just making a room smell better, we show her the value we place on her femininity.

Mothers, it is important that you express the passionate side of yourselves so your daughters can learn that passion is okay. There is nothing more dull than a cheerless, passionless home. Share about romance and love, about sympathy and caring, about what is noble and good. Read good books with female heroines and talk about them, such as *Anne of Green Gables, Christy, Jane Eyre,* and *Pride and Prejudice.* Watch good movies together and talk about them. Mothers need to have fun with their daughters, showing their own enjoyment of their womanhood. They need to express emotion and passion in a way that teaches their daughters that it is exciting to be a woman. And they can wisely teach the strengths and weaknesses of emotions and passions and how to express them. A mother who is secure enough in her femininity to do this makes femininity appealing to her daughter. Once femininity is given value, warmth and beauty are returned to the home. And this is the environment where young girls develop into strong, secure, feminine women who are of great value to this world.

A Few Secrets on Raising Daughters

1. Enjoy Them

Confident parents enjoy their children. Daughters are especially appreciative of their parents' affirmation. Look for opportunities to share memorable times together. Play with your daughter. Press through the walls or barriers that separate parents and daughters from having an open, enjoyable relationship. Daughters want to be heard and respected by their mothers. They want their fathers to validate their choices—in clothes, hairstyles, etc. They need their parents' approval, and daughters can feel whether there is approval in the home or not.

Sheila was so concerned about her weight, her complexion, and her clothes that it would take all day for her to get ready to go somewhere. The family was always waiting on her, so often that she started to withdraw and would rather stay home alone than try to look right. A few times she tried to be ready on time, only to have missed it somewhere with her mom telling her that she shouldn't go out in public dressed like that and her dad telling her she had on too much makeup.

Sheila just couldn't figure it out, so she started staying home, listening to music, and talking with her friends for endless hours on the phone. When her parents noticed, they decided to help Sheila by making the choice to enjoy her more and looking for opportunities to affirm her as a maturing young woman. They began complimenting her when she did things right and changed their attitudes from a guarded critical view to a view of encouragement and acceptance. At the same time, they decided to give her a little more freedom in the midst of acceptance. The experiment began.

Dad started admiring his daughter more and telling her about it. Mom started taking her shopping and sensitively directing her toward more appropriate clothes. They started letting her stay at home occasionally without any hassles and started accepting her friends with greater ease, some more than others, granted, but they made the effort. And things started to change.

Sheila started enjoying her parents more. She felt respected by them and started to care about their opinion of her. It felt good to have her parents respect her, and she wanted to keep this relationship going. She also started feeling better about herself as she enjoyed her parents' acceptance. They now have a great family, and Sheila is doing great. She's a great kid.

2. Don't Be Harsh and Critical All the Time

Sarah just couldn't make her father happy. She tried to dress the way he liked, and he wouldn't notice. She tried to clean up the house or her room and he wouldn't notice. Actually, it felt to her like everything she did was wrong. So she was tempted to give up.

One day while at school, one of the teachers noticed Sarah in distress. She asked about it, and Sarah told the story of her dad griping and complaining all the time. She explained that she loved him and appreciated his hard work, but he seemed to have anger in his eyes when he looked at her, and when he said something nice to her, it was usually followed with something critical, embarrassing, or demanding. Sarah just wanted him to be nice.

The teacher encouraged Sarah to volunteer to be in the school play, with the hope that maybe her dad would appreciate her after a great performance at school. Sarah said she would think about it but hated the thought of being on stage reciting lines with a critical father in the audience. She was afraid of the risk. She wanted to do the play, she wanted to be with her friends, she wanted to excel at school, but she couldn't stand another broken heart. She didn't want to face one more critical comment and another night of tears alone in her room.

Families like Sarah's have a hard time raising great kids because fear keeps their kids from trying. We regularly see kids doing great work at school or at church until their parents walk in, and then they melt. Parents, this is our chance to be their best friend, not a critic or a taskmaster, but a parent, a coach, a supporter, a fan.

3. Spend Time with Her (Every Day)

Commit to spend thirty minutes a day with your daughter, regardless of your present state of estrangement. Our most important relationships in the world are the relationships with our children. When we travel, we make a point to call home or write e-mails to our spouses and our children. If they aren't there, we are sure to leave a message of love. In addition, little cards, notes, or pictures are always appreciated. You'll know they are appreciated because you'll find them taped to a mirror or stuck on the refrigerator when you get home. Daughters especially love to receive expressions of affection.

Time every day, whether we are home or not, is vitally important. And with that time, connect with them by talking about the things that interest them. If they want to talk about guinea pigs, bubble gum, or a new soda pop, then that is the subject. We've had to learn about movies, bands, dances, instruments, computers, horses, dogs, cats, actors, teen idols, boys at school, and clothing styles in the last few years, and we're interested in all of it—aren't we? You bet we are! Why? Because we love our daughters.

We've also learned to be available for those times when they want to talk, which is often late at night when they get home from an activity or being out with their friends. Make a habit of inviting your teenagers into your bedroom at night before you go to bed. Talk about their day. Get their thoughts on family issues and decisions. Talk about hot news items and get their opinions. This is a great time to connect. Sometimes this is the only time your daughter will open up about something that is bothering her. Sometimes this will be the time when she wants to hear from you. Don't let her think that all her concerns "can wait until morning." The intimacy of the moment may be lost by morning. Take every opportunity you can to connect positively.

4. Give Her Confidence

When we believe in and support our daughters, training them to be honorable and trusting them to make wise decisions, they gain a beautiful, graceful confidence. As we invest in our daughters by helping them learn to think through issues, to learn why they should dress modestly and live with honor and integrity, our daughters learn a confidence that will carry them through life with strength. Help your daughter develop problem-solving skills so that she does not have to feel totally helpless and dependent on a man. Don't rescue her from every situation—guide her gently and let her find her way.

5. Recognize Her Strengths

Find your daughter's interests and help her develop skills in those areas. It doesn't matter what area your daughter develops expertise in, whether it is in playing a musical instrument, playing sports, or breeding guinea pigs—having confidence in one area increases confidence in other areas. Compliment her on her achievements. Appreciate that her strengths may be different than yours and enjoy that about her.

We are friends with a couple who have a teenager named Ashley. Ashley's mother is very proper and cautious about how she comes across to other people. She guards her words and tries to be kind and polite at all times. Ashley, on the other hand, is very open with her thoughts and feelings and doesn't care what people think about what she says. At first her mother was appalled at Ashley's brashness, which she interpreted as being inconsiderate, and she was constantly correcting this horrible personality trait. But over time, Ashley's mother began to see that although this trait was a little rough around the edges, her daughter's frankness was refreshing both to her and others and generally led to exciting and interesting conversation. She began to appreciate this strength she found in her daughter and began to help her develop it better. As it turned out, she found she could learn as much from her daughter's strengths as her daughter could learn from hers.

6. Build Her Spirit By Modeling a Great Family Life

Build your daughter's spirit by giving her a healthy family. Let her see your affection for each other as you hold hands, hug, and kiss. Let her see and hear that you love each other. This will give her a dream for her future. It will also give her security. Do not criticize your spouse in front of your children. Do not gripe and complain about the cost of everything or voice regrets about how many children you have or the kind of job you have and what you can't afford. Do not be verbally abusive to your spouse or daughter. This teaches the daughter that a spouse has the right to be abusive in this way. It tears down her dream.

Attend church as a family. Let your daughter see you worship God and let her see you trust in someone bigger than yourself. Teach her that there is security in family love, but even we can't control everything in our lives. Just let her see you sincerely doing your best to live a life of character.

7. Release Her Appropriately

Release your daughter appropriately as she grows. First, convince her of the security of your love for her. Let her know it is your delight to provide for her and protect her. Then release her in stages. If you've done your job as parents, you can trust her to make good and godly decisions with her life. If and when you release her to a husband, make sure she understands that she is still and will always be secure in your love and admiration of her, but now she must work out her marriage relationship and your home is no longer her place of provision and protection. This will be hard to do, especially during her early years of marriage. That is why you must always counsel her to marry a good man, and hopefully she will seek your guidance in doing so. Now your role in her life will be to encourage her to be a successful wife and to have a successful marriage.

If your daughter does not marry, you may continue to have a strong role in her life, to offer her counsel when she needs it. As a single woman she may continue to need to depend on her father for masculine perspective or physical help. But once again, your most important role is that of encouraging her to be a successful adult.

Our daughters bring us a different kind of blessing than our sons. It has been said that it is our daughters who take care of us in our old age. The potential is there for a rich, long-lasting, caring, and life-giving relationship. As parents, we should press on for this reward. Daughters touch our hearts in a way no one else can. When George Bush's daughter died, he began to discover the value of femininity. In a long letter to his mother, Bush painstakingly described the gaping hole that his daughter's death left in his life:

> This letter ... is kind of like a confessional ... between you and me, a mother and her little boy—now not so little, but still just as close, only when we are older, we hesitate to talk from our hearts quite as much.
>
> There is about our house a need. The running, pulsating restlessness of the four boys as they struggle to learn and grow; their athletic chests and arms and legs; their happy noises as the world embraces them ... all this wonder needs a counterpart. We need some starched, crisp frocks to go with all our torn-kneed blue jeans and helmets. We need some soft, blond hair to offset those crewcuts. We need a dollhouse to stand firm against our forts and racquets and a thousand baseball cards. We need a cut-out start to play alone while the others battle to who's "family champ." We even need someone ... who could sing the descant to "Alouette," while out-

side the scramble to catch the elusive ball aimed ever roofward but usually thudding against the screens.

We need a legitimate Christmas angel—one who doesn't have cuffs beneath the dress.

We need someone who is afraid of frogs.

We need someone to cry when I get mad—not argue.

We need a little one who can kiss without leaving egg or jam or gum.

We need a girl.

We had one once. She'd fight and cry and play and make her way just like the rest. But there was about her a certain softness.

She was patient—her hugs were just a little less wiggly.

Like them, she'd climb into sleep with me but somehow she'd fit.

She didn't boot and flip and wake me up with pug nose and mischievous eyes, a challenging quarter inch from my sleeping face.

No—she'd stand beside our bed till I felt her there. Silently and comfortably she'd put those precious, fragrant locks against my chest and fall asleep.

Her peace made me feel strong and so very important.

"My Daddy" had a caress, a certain ownership which touched a slightly different spot than the "Hi Dad" I love so much.

But she is still with us. We need her and yet we have her. We can't touch her and yet we can feel her.

We hope she'll stay in our house for a long, long time.[7]

CHAPTER
Thirteen

"But I Don't Like My Teenager Anymore!"

Having children makes one no more a parent than having a piano makes you a pianist.

MICHAEL LEVINE

CHANGING THE TAGS

During World War II, a system was developed to label men as they were brought from the battlefield into the infirmary. As they were wheeled into crude first-aid tents, wounded soldiers were given either a red, yellow, or green tag to indicate the level of medical attention required. The tag was placed in such a way that the wounded soldier could not be aware of it. The tagging system was only for the medical staff. A red tag indicated severe injuries. These patients were to be heavily medicated, and there was little the doctors could do to help them. A yellow tag represented moderate injuries and more aggressive medical attention. A yellow tag meant that the patient might survive if given the right amount of attention and God's grace. A green tag was the sign of hope. The men with green tags usually survived if treated quickly and correctly.

War legend tells us a story of a soldier for the Allies who had suffered horrible injury on the battlefield. He was brought to the infirmary and given a red tag almost immediately. He was quickly medicated and left in the corner of the first-aid tent. For hours, the man lay in a catatonic state as doctors and nurses scurried around him tending to less severely injured men.

Sometime later, an attending nurse noticed the man in the corner. She lovingly checked his vitals, replenished his anesthetics, and walked away. She stopped. Something inside her leaped. Slowly, she turned around and faced the young man's bed. Walking back toward him, she scanned the busy room to see if anyone was watching. Then, in a moment of compassion and desperation, she did the unthinkable. She reached down and pulled the red tag off the wounded man's bed and replaced it with a green tag. Her heart raced as she thought of the possible consequences of what she'd done. But the thought of this man surviving trumped her fears.

With a green tag on his bed, the wounded soldier was given the very best medical attention and, more importantly, the belief that he could survive. Consequently, he lived. Several weeks later, he limped out of the infirmary and onto a U.S. battleship bound for New York City. He was going home. He had survived a world war, massive injuries, and an infirmary death sentence. He survived because someone gave him a chance for survival. He survived because someone believed in him. He survived because someone switched his tags.

That's our job too. To switch our kids' tags.

When the system says our kids can't make it, we say they can. When the government says our kids are defective, we say they aren't. When the papers say our kids are hopeless and when society leaves them to die in the corner of the tent, we take the risk and switch their tags. We look at our kids—beaten, bruised, forgotten—and hold onto a glimmer of promise. That's what parents do. That's what mentors do. There's no greater antidote for a hurting teenager than someone who believes in them. Someone who will fight to switch their tags.

As you embark on the adventure of raising your teenagers, always take time to listen to their dreams, goals, and secret ambitions. Determine to believe in your kids no matter what. When your teen makes small, marked improvements, take notice. When your teen shows interest in a particular science, art form, or hobby, take time to understand and appreciate. When your kids show interest in things you don't see as important or worthy, find a way to encourage them while using your wisdom as a parent. Remember, the self-esteem of a teenager is a precious thing. It's one of the most fragile things in the world. If crushed, it can turn a happy, hopeful teenager into a lonely, inward person. Don't allow your words to be the sand in the machinery of your kids' dreams. Believe in them. Believe in what they can become. There are few things as powerful as the belief of a parent. It can turn a shy little boy into a Winston Churchill. It can turn an insecure artist into a Walt Disney. It can turn a fumbling athlete into a Michael Jordan. Who lives in your house? A president? A world-class figure skater? A highly respected attorney? It might be up to you. Determine today to change their tags.

"YEAH, BUT YOU DON'T KNOW *My* TEENAGER . . ."

To switch our teens' tags, we must first believe in them. Many parents struggle with their teenagers because, somewhere around fourteen years old, they suddenly become such strangers. You say goodnight to Opie, and you say good morning to Frankenstein. In these stages, your teen can seem so strange that your main concern switches from loving and enjoying them to controlling them and living long enough to tell about it. You think you've raised a monster and failed as a parent. Your teen tests the waters of individualism, experimenting with different styles, moods, habits, and friends, and you feel as though you're being hurled into parenthood's black hole. You feel like everything you've ever taught your teen has been surgically removed from their brain. When your teen is in one of these stages, there is one little gem of advice that can get you through: like them anyway. Find things to enjoy about them. Continue getting to know them. Genuinely be their friend *and* their parent, walking the balance between casually hanging out with them and correcting potentially negative behavior.

We all know that "I love you" has to be the most common phrase in our homes. No one in America is arguing over the importance of loving teenagers. But what about liking them? What about truly enjoying our teens? What about making them laugh? What about delighting in their lives? What about appreciating all their quirks, their moods, their uniqueness? Of course we love our kids, but are we capable of *liking* them?

While working with thousands of teens, we've made an informal effort to try to find the common denominator for every great kid we've met. What would that one common denominator be? Financial security? No. Both biological parents at home? No. Family dinners? Not necessarily. A healthy family faith system? Not always. A private school education? No, not even close. Even though all of these give kids great opportunity, they aren't the thing that makes kids great. The one common denominator that is consistent among all the great kids we know is that their parents like them.

Love can be abstract, but liking someone is not. The reason so many kids struggle is not because their parents don't love them but because their parents never make it obvious that they like them, like Ted's mom did for him:

> I remember that my Mom was excited when summer vacation was approaching. She was always happy whenever we had a snow day or a teacher conference day because we would be able to spend the day at home with her. No doubt we tore up the house fighting with each other, but Mom looked past those things to welcome us home. We actually believed that she liked us being at home (I wonder if it was true? We'll never know.). Dad was the same way—happy when we would be able to come to the office or go on a trip

with him. He communicated that he liked us. Neither he nor Mom ever told jokes cutting us down, making us feel embarrassed, or pawning us off on someone else. They liked having us around, and they made us feel that way. Sometimes when I'm putting my kids into bed I tell them how much I like them being my son or daughter. When I travel I e-mail them or call them. I always try to find little cards for them and always tell them that I wish they were with me. When they are on summer vacation, I take them with me whenever possible. I think this gives them courage, makes them strong, and helps them believe that other people like them too.

When we like someone, we enjoy talking with them, spending time with them, and looking for every opportunity to cross paths with them. When we see someone we like, we smile, our eyes are bright, we want to hear what they have to say, and we want to talk with them about things in their lives and tell them about things in ours. We enjoy vacationing with people we like, traveling with them, working with them, suffering with them, and growing with them. We like being with people we like. We call people we like. We e-mail them, buy them gifts, and do everything we can to profit their lives.

This same dynamic is a common ingredient in great kids. Parents who like their kids spend weekends and evenings with them. They look forward to late night conversations. They read books together, play games together, go for long walks together. Kids whose parents like them, in turn, learn to enjoy family life. They think of Mom and Dad as friends as well as authorities. They know that home is a place of security and acceptance, so they are less likely to pursue acceptance elsewhere. The downward spiral starts easily when kids find out that other kids are smarter than they are or are better looking than they are. Depending upon their response, they can begin the spiral of self-rejection. But if Dad's eyes sparkle every time he sees his kids and Mom is so pleased to have the kids home from school during vacation, the kids will automatically cope with competition, rejection, and the inevitable ridicule that comes in every person's life.

What is a boy doing when he gets into trouble in school? What is a girl doing when she wears too much makeup and too little clothing? They are looking for people who will like them. If we let them keep looking in the wrong places, they will enter into the downward spiral and destroy their lives. To keep this from happening, we must develop relationships with our kids where they know we enjoy them and that we are still their parents—we provide protection from poor choices, but we are their friends too.

Note that we are not saying that parents should like their teenagers in spite of their actions. Recently, we've swallowed the lie that tolerance and pampering are the answer for troubled kids. We've been told to appreciate our kids for "who they are," to boost their self-image, and to allow them to explore whatever lifestyle makes them happy. This sounds great, but it's deceptive. It takes the tools of discipline and instruction out of our hands, and leaves us only with empty rhetoric. Remember, happiness is not the goal in life. We can't raise great kids by trying to make them happy or avoiding struggle. Tough times in a teenager's life are part of what makes growing up great. Avoid trying to make everything easy for your teen. Some of the greatest monsters in history were tolerated too much, had woefully strong self-images, and never had anyone tell them, "No." Instead, we must create a home where Mom and Dad have a relationship with their teenagers that is both enjoyable and instructive.

"Okay, so I understand that I need to like my teen, but how do I balance the equation of friendship and strong parenting?" Good question.

FOUR WAYS TO LET YOUR KIDS KNOW YOU LIKE THEM, AND STILL BE THEIR PARENT

1. Know What You Are Communicating

The living room is alive. It's game night and Dad's friends are all jammed into the area around the TV. Like some kind of primitive ritual, the men begin to grunt as fists are plunged into the air in primal instinct. As the night wears on, the room becomes more and more alive. The clan of men is feeding on the energy transferred from the twenty-seven-inch box in the front of the room. Deep laughter, slaps on the back, and deafening cheers fill the room as the men enjoy the big game. They are having the time of their lives.

Far in the back of the room, your young boy sits. Watching, listening, assimilating. The fifteen-year-old boy is deciding who he will become. What should make him laugh. What he should wear. How he should act. Who he should befriend.

The colors whir by like an old carousel at the county fair. Your daughter laughs and pushes you as you walk through the mall trying to stay in step with each other like some funny rerun of *Laverne and Shirley*. Mother and daughter. Together. That magical feeling fills the air that only occurs when a mother and daughter enter into the hallowed halls of Dillards. That feeling that men will never understand. After hours of laughing, throwing clothes over the dressing room door, and searching for that perfect pair of jeans, the two are like one.

As a mom, you might never notice it, but it always happens. She's watching and learning. How you dress, how you laugh, how you shop. You set for your daughter the value of makeup versus the value of talent. The value of clothes versus the value of character.

As boys and girls grow up to become teenagers, carefully consider what you communicate as valuable and important. In every situation, your teens will be assimilating and forming their own values, so take the opportunity to model an appropriate lifestyle. Simple activities like watching sports and going shopping can become awesome parenting tools if you'll just consider what your teen might be learning.

2. Mirror, Mirror: Enjoy Their Physical Appearance, and Help Them Enjoy It

Life is a mirror and will reflect back to the thinker what he thinks into it.

ERNEST HOLMES

Self-image sets the boundaries of individual accomplishment.
MAXWELL MALTZ

If you expect nothing, you're apt to be surprised. You'll get it.
MALCOLM FORBES

What do your kids see when they look in the mirror? Think of the young teenager who sees only a fragment of the girl she used to be. Instead of the happy little girl who was content to sit on Daddy's lap and laugh at his mustache, now she is consumed with thoughts of herself as ugly, fat, and worthless. Why? Maybe it's because Daddy stopped telling his little girl how pretty she was. Maybe he stopped delighting in his daughter's beauty. Think of the boy who looks into the mirror and sees the guy who can't seem to do anything right. He can't make the team, can't get the girl, can't pass the class. When did he stop believing his mom telling him he could do anything? When did Mom stop telling him he could?

As our kids grow up, the power of words, positive and negative, is intensified. With this in mind, make an extra effort to encourage your kids and encourage them to believe in themselves. The old saying, "If you think you are, you are," is true. There's also a song that says, "Who told you you weren't beautiful?" Let's not be guilty of neglecting to verbally encourage our kids. Make your confidence in your teen contagious, so when they look in the mirror they see how beautiful they really are.

3. Communicate Love Often

As we prepared to write this book, we spent a considerable amount of time researching the notable essays and books on the topic of raising kids. In the process, we were shocked to discover that, of the dozens of books and periodicals we read, we found only two that mentioned the importance of love in raising a teenager.

In the nineties, affection is a lot more accepted than in generations past. In our society, it's not at all odd for a dad to hug his son or for a mom to embrace her daughter. As your kids grow up through the teenage years, affection is an important ingredient in their success. Teens need affection and love to become great kids. Recent research actually connects successful adults with the amount of affection they received as kids. Children who are physically neglected generally grow into more inward, less successful adults, and well-hugged children have a lot better chance to become happy, healthy people.

Letters or notes aptly written communicate love in a way that will be remembered and appreciated. You don't have to be a Shakespeare or Hemingway to take a few minutes to tell your teen that you love them. A few weeks ago, John was cleaning his garage when he stopped at a small box filled with wrinkled and folded notes and cards. He sat and opened the old cards and was transported back in time to a place called "teenagerdom." John read a note Dad sent on his sixteenth birthday and letters from Mom sent to him when he was on an overseas trip to the Philippines. The words on the letters and cards jumped off the pages and into his heart as a reminder of the ones who believed. The ones who switched the tags in his life.

A few small words that made a big difference. Take time to write to your kids. After all, one day you'll want them to write to you too.

4. The Cat's In the Cradle—Spend Time

Today, the most valuable resource we have is time, not money or things. There's no better way to communicate to our kids that we love them than to give them some of our valuable time. Often our temptation is to shove money or things at our kids in lieu of time, but it will always fall short. Remember Dylan and Eric of the Columbine incident were both from middle- to upper-class families? They had nice clothes and expensive cars. But no amount of money could buy the time that may have been lost between them and their parents. Reports have indicated that the parents saw no warning signs. Why? Maybe it was because they failed to offer their kids the one thing that really makes a difference—time.

We've all seen the made-for-TV movies about the deadbeat dad who's too busy at the office to make the Little League game or the fast-paced mom who can't find time to really meet her own kids. The reality and gravity of the loss of time spent with our kids is real. A couple of generations ago, society was different, the pace was slower, and homes were still built with dining rooms. Today, we have shifted our lives into hyper-drive as we scurry off to work, quickly dropping our kids off at day care or football practice. We've adopted a "pass in the night" mentality of parenting, and yet we wonder why our kids are distant and disconnected. They need time. They need you. If the choice is a dollar earned or a minute spent, take the minute. It's an investment that will reward you with dividends of love and relationship for the rest of your life.

The reality of parenting is that it requires more than just advice, more than just parenting books, more than just herding your kids through the house until they leave for college. Parenting requires your heart, your soul. It requires your life. It asks you to look at that strange kid in his or her messy bedroom and recommit to being the best parent you can be. It requires the steadfast faith of that compassionate nurse in the World War II infirmary—a faith that takes the hopeless and gives them hope.

Evan was shoved deep in the corner of the infirmary of life, waiting to die. At sixteen, he should have been enjoying learning to drive, working at his first job, and nervously waiting for his first real date. But he wasn't. Evan had been dealt a rotten hand in the game of life. His parents split up when he was ten after a long, heartbreaking divorce settlement case. The court landed him with his father, and Evan walked into a living hell. Something snapped in his dad after the divorce was final. His entire personality changed. Once Evan and his dad would sit on the edge of the old dock lazily fishing for that elusive ten-pound bass. Now Evan sat alone every night waiting for his dad to burst in the door after a night of drinking with his new buddies. His dad's sharp words about grades, chores, and sports achievement rang through the house every week. The hands that once taught Evan to use a fishing reel now taught him not to talk back. Evan sunk deep into the painful world of both verbal and physical abuse at the hands of a sad and frustrated dad.

Then, Mrs. Elliott walked into Evan's life. One Sunday morning, Evan's best friend, Andy, invited him to attend church. Evan accepted the invitation and met the kindly old lady in the foyer of the church. Mrs. Elliott had heard Evan's story from a mutual friend. Over the next few months, Mrs. Elliott all but adopted Evan. Without ever telling him why, she simply became his friend. That's it. No preaching or reforming, just love. And something happened. The inward, sad boy slowly returned to his once-happy self. The boy without hope became an honor student. Today, as a freshman in medical school, Evan still writes Mrs. Elliott. His words are few. "Thank you for believing in me." Mrs. Elliott didn't have a desk or a degree, she just believed in Evan. She changed the tag.

The past thirty years of psychology have taught us that if we practice tolerance and mutual respect with our teens, we will produce healthy, happy kids. It hasn't worked. Certainly, respect is important, but so are boundaries, listening, and appropriate freedom. Brass tacks. The bottom line. It really all comes down to this: Love your kids. Really love them. Like Jesus did. If you do, you'll see your house transformed from a place of scared parents and average kids to a gallery of life featuring confident parents and exceptional teens.

Notes

CHAPTER ONE: KIDS IN TROUBLE

1. Nancy Gibbs (May 3, 1999). "In Sorrow and Disbelief." [1]. *Time*. [HTTP]. Available: http://cgi.pathfinder.com/time/magazine/articles/0,3266,23541–3,00.html [7/8/99].

CHAPTER THREE: MOLD THEIR PURPOSE: THE PASSPORT TO GREAT LIVES

2. Stephen R. Covey, *The 7 Habits of Highly Effective Families* (New York: Golden Books, 1998), 72.

CHAPTER FOUR: GUARD THEIR MINDS: AIM THE LAMP

3. Daniel Okrent, "Raising Kids Online: What Can Parents Do?" *Time*. Vol. 153, No. 18. (May 10, 1999), 43.

CHAPTER FIVE: SHAPE THEIR CHARACTER: THE TEN COMMANDMENTS FOR PARENTS OF TEENS

4. Michael Gurian, *A Fine Young Man* (New York: Tarcher/Putnam, 1998), 211.

CHAPTER TEN: CHURCH: HOW DOES FAITH FIT IN?

5. Dallas Willard, *The Divine Conspiracy* (New York: HarperCollins, 1998), 12.

CHAPTER ELEVEN: BOYS INTO MEN

6. William Pollack, *Real Boys* (New York: Henry Holt, 1998), 181, 185.

CHAPTER TWELVE: GIRLS INTO WOMEN

7. George Bush, quoted in Bush, Barbara, *Barbara Bush: A Memoir* (St. Martin's Paperbacks: New York, 1994), 51-52.